MW01097706

ROW, ROW, ROW YOUR BOAT

Memoirs of an Admiral's Wife

PATRICIA LINDER

ISBN: 1-4033-6753-1 (e-book)
ISBN: 1-4033-6754-X (Paperback)

Library of Congress Control Number: 2002111804

This book is printed on acid free paper.

Printed in the United States of America
Bloomington, IN

1stBooks – rev. 10/23/02

To Jamey and Jeff
Who shared their strengths with me
When I needed them most.

Acknowledgements

I wish to thank those who encouraged me and never failed to ask, "How's the book coming?" You know who you are.

My loving appreciation to the Wynns, Martha and Jack, who lived the life and helped with memories that needed validating and who, after thirty-seven years, could still weep over the days of Vietnam.

Hon. Roger Zion took the time to read and sanction the use of passages that told of the efforts generated in his Congressional office on behalf of the Prisoners of War and Missing in Action. My heartfelt thanks.

My editor, Carna Miller for her unending patience and good humor.

To my agent Nancy Ellis, who kept the faith and helped me do the same.

And finally, my husband Jim, who never really left the flight deck, and so thoughtfully relinquished his Flight Logs that provided cu-and-dried testimonies to perilous times. Without his expertise and patience, this story would still be in the back of my mind.

ROW, ROW, ROW YOUR BOAT

Memoirs of an Admiral's Wife

PATRICIA LINDER

I will go back to the great sweet mother,
Mother and lover of men, the sea.

Swinburne

This is as I remember it and because perceptions differ, I have changed some of the names to protect and preserve friendships.

PROLOGUE

Vietnam 1965

*The phone on the Chaplain's desk rang softly and
excusing himself, he turned from me to answer it.
After a moment of silence as he listened, he glanced at me,
then swung his chair around to face the wall.
I waited in the quiet room. Slowly, he turned back to
face his desk. Avoiding my eyes, he spoke carefully,
"Mrs. Linder, they have just reported that your husband,
Commander Linder has been shot down over Hanoi."*

Virginia Beach, Virginia

Patricia Linder

CHAPTER ONE

Two years later, San Diego, California, October 24, 1967

Sitting there in the soft October night, I wondered how in the name of God would I be able to do what I must. The car was a tight little island that sheltered me from the hardness of a world I had voluntarily taken on. As a bride, it had looked exciting and as a bride, I was willing to take my lumps for the man I had promised to love and obey. In 1949, they still said, "obey". But nothing had prepared me for this. Men were down over enemy territory and as the Commanding Officer's wife, I must tell their wives and children.

There, but for the grace of God, go I.

Virginia Beach, four months earlier

The Vietnam War was three years old when my husband Jim returned to it for the second time. He told me of his new orders over lunch at the Pickle Factory, just down the street from BUPERS (Bureau of Personnel) in Washington D.C. The restaurant was a favorite haunt for naval officers and I waved to several we knew on our way to an empty table.

Something was up. There was a controlled tenseness about Jim. I could feel the coiled spring of excitement that was ready to snap. Orders were expected and we had made the four -hour drive from Virginia Beach to Washington early in the morning, planning to return the same night. While he visited BUPERS, I shopped in the Marine Exchange, close by. Normally, I would have enjoyed my chance to find new and different things. But uneasiness had settled on me and despite the warm, fall day, I felt cold. My feet weren't interested in moving and although my fingers touched the silk of a blouse, I forgot to look down at it. Instead, my eyes were fastened on the door. In a short while, our lives would change again. Orders are orders and wherever they wanted us, we would go. The coldness in my soul tried to warn me, but my mind simply shut down on the possibility of another Vietnam combat tour.

At the Pickle Factory, we studied the menu, discussed the pros and cons of various sandwiches and I waited. My marriage had been one of waiting and from that, had come control. Somewhere along the way during those eighteen years, I learned how to shift my mind into neutral. It was a survival technique that gave me time to fashion my reactions.

"Patti, they've given me an Air Group." It was surgically blunt. In the silence that followed, I rationalized that aircraft carriers with air groups went east to the Mediterranean as well as west to Vietnam. I looked into his face and saw excitement and pride and knew it was not the Mediterranean. He would be returning to combat over the missile laden skies of North Vietnam. The control I was so proud of deserted me and with tears streaming down my face, I fled to the ladies' room. Eighteen years, a Navy wife and I'm cowering in a booth, pounding my fist against the tile wall.

It took some time, but eventually I returned to the table, head down – not wanting to see the curious glances of the naval officers who always assume wives don't make waves. Dammit, of course we make waves. We're human beings, not robots. We just don't do it in public unless we lose control and God knows I've just lost control.

Jim stood, jaw hard and fire in his eyes. "What was that all about? I thought you would be pleased. You know how I've always hoped I'd get an Air Group."

Good for the career. To hell with the career, I just want him alive.

We rented our new home, told our children they would be changing schools again and driving two cars, headed to California. Thanks to a state of shock, it was a quiet trip. Our sixteen year-old daughter's only comment was, "Dad, I give up." Three high schools in two years and eight moves besides had left her punchy. She had lost her will to adjust.

San Diego, 1967

His Air Group boarded the aircraft carrier; Coral Sea and left San Francisco for combat that by now was honed to a sharp edge. Both sides knew what they were doing and how to do it better than ever before. That particularly applied to the enemy. Their surface-to-air missiles (SAMS), were more numerous and accurate. With radar controlled anti-aircraft fire, the Viet Cong cut a swath through our pilots. Russian Mig intercept planes lay in wait as soon as they launched from the ship and flew toward the mainland. On bombing runs, if the pilot flew below 1,000 feet, planes were lost from small arms fire. The wonder is that anyone came back at all.

Many did not.

The wives of these men filled out forms asking that they designate whom they wished to tell them if their husbands were shot down. Some said the Chaplain; a few, their closest friend if they were in the area. I found my name on the forms more often than I wished. They knew I would receive the information first and further word would come more quickly through the Commanding Officer's wife. They also knew I cared a great deal about every one of them. Obediently, they followed the directions on the bureaucratic sheets of paper that could change their lives.

Back in the early days, when I was a new Navy wife learning my lessons like a good girl, a C.O.s wife gave me a piece of advice.

"Don't bother your husband with family problems when he's flying. It will break his concentration. There's nothing he can do about it anyway." What she was saying in effect was, if you tell your husband your problems, he will probably crash and burn and it will be your fault. So here I was with death, destruction and teen-age problems on my hands but nobody to talk to. 'It's lonely at the top' became more than a cliché.

My small -town Midwestern upbringing had taught me that at the end of every week, was church. Able to think of other things I would rather do, I found I was not particularly religious as a child. My parents, due to the monetary restrictions of the Great Depression and the absolute conviction of college educations for their three children, relied on the church to give them the strength to get through the next week.

San Diego was rife with churches and many of them were against the war. It was not a passive opinion. Protestors with anti-Vietnam slogans were allowed to march into Sunday morning services and inflammatory sermons were preached to ambivalent congregations. At the first church we attended after moving in, we as a family, took our seats, found the hymn numbers and settled in to enjoy the charisma of quiet.

From the pulpit, the minister who had just welcomed us into 'his' church launched into a sermon that identified Jim, because of his profession, as a murderer of Vietnamese children. Our children were in shock as we rose and left that church, never to return. So much for spiritual support.

October 24th 1967

"Word is just in on a massive air strike over North Vietnam. Pilots on the aircraft carrier, Coral Sea launched their planes yesterday afternoon for raids on the Phuc Yen Airfield, northwest of Hanoi. Heavy losses from enemy SAM missile sites in that area were reported."

The children and I were on our way to another church for a second try when the voice with a news bulletin, interrupted the music on the car radio. I clicked off as soon as I realized what he was saying, but the children had heard. It was their father's Air Group and we knew

7

he was in combat on Yankee Station. In the parking lot, we sat silently, each sorting through our thoughts.

"Children, it's Dad's Air Group, but that doesn't mean it's Dad. We don't know who was leading the strike and it's more than likely he was on the Bridge with the Air Boss than flying. Let's not borrow trouble. We'll go on to church, then right home and wait to hear." Knowing Jim, he was leading the strike and my hands were icy cold as I opened the car door.

Church was a blur.

Jamey refused to sing or read the responses and Jeff just sat and stared at the stained glass window. At home, I tried to talk to our daughter, but she answered me with angry words I have never forgotten.

"Mom, don't try to understand me. Just be there when I need you."

Jeff went to his room and I could hear the soft, sad strains of the latest song he had written as he bent over his guitar. We all waited for the phone to ring.

At seven o'clock that night, a friend in Communications called.

"Pat, this is a heads up call. There are a lot of planes down in Jim's Air Group and you will probably be hearing from the C.O. of Miramar soon. Just wanted to give you a little advance notice in case you need it." Good man and a God-given friend.

My hand stuck to the phone and I realized my palms were wet. I knew what was ahead. The term is 'next of kin' and I would be facing them in a few hours.

The phone rang again with a request for my presence at the Commanding Officer's Quarters at Miramar Naval Air Station. I talked with the children, explaining what was happening, and tried to prepare them for the wait ahead.

"Kiddoes, how about a little conference in my room. I've just had a call, asking me to drive out to Miramar to meet with the C.O. of the Base. There have been some casualties in Dad's Air Group, but he's all right or they would be here instead of asking me to go there." Death again, and they knew they must deal with it.

As we sat on the bed I looked at the faces of our children – Jamey, just seventeen and Jeff, fourteen. They were wise beyond their ages, bright, intelligent, but with a stillness about them, as if they were waiting. I knew the feeling well. Our lives as a family had been one of waiting. Waiting for the one person who made our family whole. Now, there was the element of fear that shadowed the eyes that met mine and I silently asked God not to let it show in my own.

Jeff looked toward the window, his angular face profiled against the darkness outside. His trademark lock of dark blonde hair fell over his forehead. "Mom, it's night out there and Miramar's a long way to drive. Will you be okay, going alone?"

"Yes, darling. I'll lock my doors and drive the speed limit. If it will make you feel better, I won't go the canyon road. I'll stick to the main freeway."

He nodded, relieved.

Jamey looked at her hand as it smoothed the coverlet on the bed. The sadness on her face was like a mask, but I knew that underneath

9

lay the warm, glowing smile of a beautiful girl and I vowed at that moment to do all I could to restore it.

She spoke softly, "Mom, will you call if it's Dad?"

"Jamey dear, it won't be your father. And I'll be back with you and Jeff as soon as they let me go. Besides, you know we don't handle important things with a phone call. If either of you have homework, try to finish it. I promise to call from the C.O.'s house so you'll know I made it out there safely."

Knowing full well that if I put my arms around them, I would break, our goodbye was casual. They needed me strong. It would be a long night for all of us.

Several days before, Secretary of Defense Robert McNamara, had released to the American press the information that the U.S. would be bombing Hanoi for the first time. It was the media's war and they had a gluttonous appetite. The enemy read the same papers we did. They prepared as they had never prepared before and the carnage began.

Almost an entire squadron was blown out of the sky.

With my thoughts in turmoil; I drove into the Naval Air Station and found my way to the CO's house after the long, dark drive to Miramar. Many cars were parked along the street. Ushered into the low, sprawling Spanish-style house, I saw men in uniform, their faces grave, crowded into the living room. The CO's wife gently guided me to a rocking chair and asked me to sit down.

Something was not right.

Her voice was low and soft as she said, "Pat, we've just had word that Jim has been shot down, along with several other pilots. The message came in when you were on your way here." Her hand stayed on my arm.

I shifted my mind into neutral and let the control take over. It didn't matter what she said, my answer was already formed. From somewhere inside of me, certainty made me respond. "No, he hasn't. Will somebody please call and confirm?"

Shocked silence and startled glances settled on me and briefly, I wondered if the 'rules' stated, 'Thou shalt not question.'

It had happened again. It was the same message I received in the Chaplain's office, nineteen months ago and a continent away. As I requested, the call was made and as before, the message of the report was a mistake in communications. If I had any nerves left, they would have shorted out at that moment. But I knew somehow, Jim was still alive and there was work to be done.

I called the children immediately, and the relief in Jamey's voice was like a song. The Chaplains, doctors and Casualty Assistance Officers discussed with me the plan for notifying the wives of their losses. I knew we would find some of them at the Sears store that night, attending a home decorating class. A Squadron CO was down and his wife was a particular friend of mine. The CACO officers and the Chaplains would tell the rest. I took the doctor with me, as one of the girls was expecting her first baby in two weeks.

I've tried to forget that night, but faces are engraved on my memory. The words 'courage' and 'strength' are familiar and well worn. Yet, they define those women. Sitting in a dark car in a parking lot, telling a young girl that her husband is gone – her life changed forever and offering whatever I had to get her through the initial shock, gave me a glimpse into the amazing ability of a Navy wife to abide. The quick denial, only to be followed by the reality of acceptance, was testimony to the fearless understanding of their husbands' profession. Even at such a moment, pride in their men was as tangible as their grief. I felt honored to be one of them.

The night was endless. As each one was told, I knew I must go on to another. The ones at home meant children to consider. I wondered how the Chaplains could do this over and over without breaking. Our reality was *now* – *our* husbands, *our* children, *our* lives and *our* pain. These women would deal with it in their own way, knowing full well that ahead, lay months and years of uncertainty, frustration and fear, and in some cases, the finality of death.

Men fight, women grieve.

CHAPTER TWO

Row, row, row your boat
Gently down the stream.
Merrily, merrily, merrily, merrily
Life is but a dream.

Child's song

I freely admit a man in a uniform has always beguiled me. They look so neat, tidy, washed behind the ears and respectful. And if they don't know you too well, they will even hold the door open for you. Of course, that was before Women's Lib.

Athens, Greece, seven years later

The Greek sun was warm on our shoulders, and the Greek sand under our toes, began the process of a sabbatical, brief though it may be. The tiny Pirreus restaurant with its rickety tables on a simple patio and the best calamari in Greece, made the perfect backdrop for what lay in front of us. Small fishing boats were pulled up on the beach with fishermen repairing their nets. Beyond was a five -mile stretch of the sparkling Aegean Sea; to the left, the sprawling ancient city of Athens. I found it hard to believe this small—town Iowa girl felt so at home in such a rocky, hard land.

13

Squinting my eyes, I could see the aircraft carrier Forrestal as it lay at anchor, five miles out. This ship had been my husband's command, his home and responsibility for the past two years. Quiet and mighty, looking every inch the lethal war machine it was, even in peaceful times, it stood guard over this friendly NATO country. That air of force, that feeling of supremacy, invulnerability and the sheer size of the great gray beast made the viewer shrink in proportion.

Shame on me.

No man who had ever served on board such a ship would ever call it a beast. But I was a wife and instead of a mistress, my husband had a ship.

For the unknowing, a mistress is easier to deal with.

My contented reverie was broken when Jim opened his eyes, stretched, then unfolded his tall, slim frame and walked slowly down to the sea's edge where a wiry, little fisherman sat on the warm sand next to his tiny, blue rowboat, examining his net for tears. Hunching his shoulders, Jim squatted beside him and with many gestures, a few words with his wallet in hand, struck a deal. For what, I hadn't a clue. He returned, smiling.

"On your feet, old girl. We're about to take a boat ride."

Being a man of few words, he offered no more and I regretfully left my chair, picked up my shoes and without question, walked to the water's edge.

To hear is to obey. One doesn't live with the military for twenty-five years without learning the basics.

14

"Are we swimming out to the ship or just soaking our feet in the Aegean?" I hoped for the foot -soak because it felt so good.

The little fisherman with dark skin like tanned leather, smiled solemnly and tiny wrinkles creased every inch of his face. Climbing into his boat, he motioned us in. He was barefooted, but his feet were so callused, they looked like shoes. His wiry body bent to the oars with arms that were nothing but muscle and we settled into place for an afternoon on the Aegean Sea.

As we cast off, I felt the stress of the past few days begin to recede. The weary acceptance of the continual lack of my husband's presence, coupled with the knowledge of what was expected of me as his wife, slipped away and we were just two people, alone. I looked forward to the moments we could talk to each other without the shrill screech of the bosun's whistle or the thunder of metal on metal as the business of moving planes onto the fight deck continued unabated. Not that I minded those sounds. Twenty-five years of aircraft carriers had left me with a deep, abiding respect and a visceral thrill each time I walked their length. In my early years as a Navy wife, looking up at the towering mass of steel as it sat in its berth, I imagined what it was saying to me.

"Shape up, lady, or ship out."

And I was just young enough to say, *"YES SIR!"*

But time had given me the edge of experience and now, when my five foot-two- inch frame faced the steel-eyed behemoth, I spoke with authority.

"If you say so, you big, gray bully, but on my terms only. Because I've *earned* it."

Athens shimmered in the distance with its curving coastline wearing the frosting of low, white Greek buildings and homes. But it was the sea that had entered my bloodstream and become a part of me. Now I sat in a tiny boat, bobbing on its beauty and wondered what came next.

"I feel a bit like Wynkum, Blynkum and Nod. Any hints on where we're going?"

Jim had that 'I'm going to surprise you' look on his face. "We're headed out to the Forrestal for my final inspection."

I was appalled. This little fisherman had five miles to row with two people in his boat, plus the distance around an aircraft carrier, the length of three football fields, then five miles back.

"Dear, can he row that far without getting a hernia?"

"When I pulled out my wallet, he said he could."

I subsided, left the impassive rower to his strokes and studied my husband.

Although he had shed his uniform for the casual shirt and trousers, as he sat relaxed in the little boat, his shoulders never lost their 'brace'. It was the stance of a Naval Academy Midshipman learned over a four-year period of time and it had become a part of him. It suggested pride and determination with a jaw to match. His angular face was tanned from long days at sea. The vertical lines between his brows spoke of the constant tension of responsibility, but the light in his amber eyes spoke of the incredible fun of it all.

It had indeed, been quite a day. Jim turned over the ship he loved to its next Captain. The Change of Command, with his officers, crew and friends from various parts of Europe was held on the hangar deck of the huge carrier. Behind the ceremonial stage were partially closed doors, thirty feet high and nearly two feet thick. Beyond, planes waited for their elevator ride to the catapults. Seated in the audience place of honor, I saw, high above our heads, the colorful NATO flags that gave fleeting glimpses of the steel beams that made up the intricate support system of the flight deck. This was the home to thundering plane launches, squealing, snapping cables, crouched and running men dodging the white hot inferno eyes of jet exhausts -- undeniably, one of the most dangerously exciting spots on earth, if your nerves can stand it. Below us, were the eight levels that housed this city of people. From bakery to boilers, its steel hull sheltered, protected and moved the thousands of men and planes to their assigned destinations. I had witnessed it all during the past two years.

An aircraft carrier was an alien world for a woman in 1974. I was the intruder, the one who might be in the way at a crucial moment of operations. The feeling of irrelevancy and unease never left me.

For the Change of Command, speeches were made, but my husband, the outgoing Commanding Officer, had lost his voice due, the Flight Surgeon told us, to the tremendous strain that goes with passing along a command. I knew better. This man simply didn't trust himself to say goodbye to the two best years of his life.

They had been good for me, too. With our children grown and gone, I spent those two years, following him around the

Mediterranean, intent on catching up on twenty-three years of separations during which our marriage had become a series of brief encounters that left emotions raw with unanswered questions. Only seeing my husband when the Forrestal was in port and, when he was gone, hauling heavy suitcases, sleeping in hostels and eating one meal a day because of dwindling finances had been worth it. The sight of Jim's ship on the horizon as it slipped silently into anchor position, was compensation enough.

A three-star Admiral had dubbed the wives who followed the ships, 'Seagulls'.

"Thank you, Admiral for comparing us to something so graceful and soaring." Silently, I added, 'Do some research, old dear. Seagulls follow a ship for garbage. That is not why we're here.'

A Carrier Command was a unique and prestigious assignment, given to only a select few. My pride in his ability to withstand the tremendous pressures was tangible.

Tangible but tempered.

I saw little of him and the phrase, 'If the Navy had wanted a man to have a wife and family, it would have issued them', was coined to keep the wife firmly in her place. Sometimes it worked, sometimes it didn't. I was one of the rebels, determined to have it all – a husband satisfied with his career and a good marriage in spite of it.

But his day would not end with the speeches of a Change of Command.

"Patti, we've had to cancel my reception at the Hilton and move it aboard ship." His voice was raspy with tension and I wondered how long it would last.

"What's happened?" As if I didn't know.

"New orders. The ship has to leave at midnight." Nothing more. I had no need to know why. "We'll do it in the Officers' Wardroom, following the ceremony, then you and I are off on our own Island cruise." It was our twenty-fifth anniversary and our gift to each other was a lazy tour of the Greek Islands.

Departure orders meant everyone should remain aboard ship.

Everyone but us.

In the wardroom, Jim reluctantly said goodbye to the officers who had served under his command and turned to me for his new coat that lay over my arm. On it were the braid and stars of the rank of Rear Admiral and, as a visiting Admiral held the coat, Jim shrugged into it, taking the hat that indicated the same rank and then shook his hand. Twenty-five years in the making, my Admiral looked down for a moment, then moved to me for my approval. I let the pride I felt for him show. To my credit, I did not look back on the family sacrifices that went into this moment. So far, our family had survived.

Down the long row of officers who formed the aisle to the Quarterdeck, down the ladder to the barge below, we were piped off the ship with honors and as a last salute, the men of the Forrestal lined the rail to say goodbye to their Captain, now Admiral. Jim, ramrod straight, returned the salute. I wasn't sure we would get through it, so much had gone into those past two years of command. But there were new orders in hand with new responsibilities and challenges for each of us. It was the pattern of a career.

There would be no time alone for a quiet talk that sunny afternoon of our twenty-fifth anniversary. He was asleep. Exhaustion etched his face, and I wished I could ease away the lines that three wars and numerous commands had placed there. His was a face of strength, even in sleep. I thought of him as a dark-haired young boy in high school, tall, lean and lanky with a shy smile and long-lashed amber eyes sobered by a war that would begin his manhood.

I had known him since those school days. After high school graduation, two things happened. He joined the Navy, not to see the world, but to serve on a submarine chaser off Virginia, hunting the dark, coastal waters for the German submarines of World War II. Loaded troop ships left the Norfolk harbor for Europe, only to be blown in two on the night's horizon. It was a dangerous job, but to a new eighteen-year-old sailor, it was combat and his first blooding ground. Heady stuff.

The other happening of some consequence was our engagement, destined to last five years before the Naval Academy would give its sanction and allow its new Ensign the freedom to finally marry. With college behind us, new officer's bars on his shoulder, we entered the world of Navy life and even then, he knew he was where he belonged. The sea was his choice and it had brought him to this warm afternoon on the Agean.

Getting more sunburned by the minute, in a little blue rowboat, the new Admiral headed for his final inspection of the Forrestal.

CHAPTER THREE

Norfolk, Virginia 1949

The hand snaked under the canvas flap, softly patting the door, seeking the handle. The rain pounded on the roof of our Jeepster as I waited at the stoplight. The wipers slapped across the windshield, but made little difference with the pouring down rain.

I had spent the afternoon in downtown Norfolk, Virginia with a visit to the Singer Sewing Machine Shop for needle and thread to make a blouse; Ensign's pay left little for shopping trips in department stores. After a movie, I planned on an early dinner in some small restaurant -- better than yesterday's bologna at the kitchen table. My new Ensign husband was aboard the aircraft carrier Franklin D. Roosevelt off the coast of Virginia and, as a bride of one month, I was learning to live alone.

The storm was unexpected, but I had remembered to put the canvas top up on our new yellow Jeepster and found it dry and waiting for me when I made my dash from the theatre. Because of the storm, I chose to forgo dinner and try to find my way back to our rented house. With the many distractions claiming my attention at that particular intersection; traffic, the pounding of the rain and the glare from the slick streets, I turned my head to the right to double check the opposite stoplight. In that same moment I saw the hand. It had nearly made contact with the door handle.

Without conscious thought, I stepped on the gas pedal, running the red light. – as did the owner of the now disappearing hand.

21

Because of the solid wall of water, I could not tell in the rear-view mirror if he was standing up or lying down and nothing short of an appearance by God himself, would make me go back to find out. Adrenaline pumping, I shot around the corner, racing for the street I knew would lead me home. But I was still new to this. A moment later, I was parked in someone's driveway, clutching the steering wheel, wondering if I would ever breathe normally again.

Husband, where are you when I need you?

'Home' was a house Jim had rented before he left -- white shingle, three stories high with a long set of steps that lead to a big front porch. I liked it. A Norfolk family that annually went to Virginia Beach for the summer was pleased to have the house occupied for the three hottest months. There was no air conditioning.

We moved in with only our suitcases, checked to make sure the plumbing worked and the electricity was on.

"Gotta run or I'll miss the ship. You'll be fine here. Lots of space, books in the living room and you're close to a movie. Be back soon. Love ya." Gone.

With a wave of his hand and the kiss of a newly married man my husband was out of sight before I knew it. Over the years, I learned never to ask for how long. My gentle childhood and girls' school training had not prepared me for the lonely fears that would always follow his abrupt departures, but my Scottish genes gave me too much pride to admit to them.

Timidly, I explored the tall white house and found that with the exception of our bedroom, one bathroom and the kitchen, every door in the house was locked. The attic and basement, would remain unknowns. My only companions in the weeks ahead were the *Collected Works of Charles Dickens.* At least he was there.

Still shaking from my encounter with the hand, I pulled into our driveway under the dripping water oaks and sat quietly, waiting for my nerves and thoughts to settle. There was a light in the basement – the basement behind the locked door. Having just moved in, I had met no neighbors. Most of the houses were dark and Baldwin Avenue appeared to be a street where *everybody* migrated to the beach in the summer. Frantically, I scanned the block. There was one light in the window of a house down the street, and   jumping from the Jeep, I made straight for it.

Pounding on the front door that finally opened, and looking very much like a wet spaniel, I sputtered out my story to a pleasant looking man with glasses on his nose, who didn't seem too shocked by what I said. He was a doctor. Without further words, he ushered me into the hall to stand, dripping on a braided rug, then walking to his desk in the study beyond, opened the drawer and withdrew a gun. Methodically, he loaded the clip.

My mouth went dry and hot though it was, my teeth were chattering. "Do you think you'll need that?" I could see the headlines in the Navy Times. 'Navy wife involved in Norfolk shooting.' Jim would not be pleased.

"After what you've told me, better safe than sorry." The cliché did not quiet my nerves.

Together, we marched under his umbrella to my front porch where he insisted I sit down on a wicker chair and tell him all that had happened. This time, coherently. My words tumbled out. When I finished, he knew everything but the hour of my birth. With kind and very sympathetic eyes, he took the house key from my shaking hand, opened the front door and the two of us crept into the dark, clammy house.

We thoroughly investigated all possibilities.

"Mrs. Linder, I think you must have hit the basement light switch here in the kitchen hallway – perhaps this morning before you went out, and there is nothing we can do about exploring the basement itself with the door locked."– which I had absolutely no interest in doing, anyway. He turned off the light.

"You know where I live if anything more happens to frighten you." He pushed his glasses up on his nose, pocketed the revolver, shook my hand and padded back through the rain to his own house. I had a neighbor.

The night was not over yet. The storm began to build. Appetite gone, I crept into the kitchen to find a butcher knife that would get me upstairs to the bedroom. Resting in the sink was the largest cockroach I had ever seen. Norfolk natives insist on calling them water bugs, but whatever it was, it looked bigger than my left foot. It was happy in the sink, so, with a shudder of distaste, I left it there.

At the head of the stairs, lightning struck a tree in the far corner of the back yard, splitting it in two, and it was then that I knew I should have returned to help the man with the sneaky hand. The wrath of

God was about to descend upon me. With the pillow over my head and the butcher knife in my fist, I spent the night apologizing for all my sins, past and future.

Chintzy McCormick lived on the corner of my street in a large, red brick Colonial house. It was impressive with fig trees, magnolias and old azalea bushes, heavy with blossoms. Chintzy, the mother of a famous Navy Admiral, liked my Jeepster. She had peered through the curtains at the little yellow car and promptly named it Buttercup. We liked each other. First, it was supper in her breakfast room, after a glass of wine in the solarium, then an hour of sitting on the couch, pouring over family photographs. Most of her family had military backgrounds and she must have sensed my apprehension about the life I had taken on.

She ran her fingers through her short silky white curls. "Now Patti dear, if you hear a shotgun blast from time to time, don't be frightened, it's only me. My neighbor likes to steal the figs off my tree and I just put my gun out the window and fire." She looked heavenward. "Up."

"Mrs. McCormick, why do you have a gun?" That was two I knew of in the same block.

"Oh, it was my husband's." She grinned. "Call me Chintzy. Everybody does. He bought it during Prohibition and it was my job to sit on the stairs with it across my knees when he was making his brew in the bathtub. Revenuers, you know."

25

I didn't doubt it for a minute. I had seen the pictures in the family album.

Chintzy was my treasure. Instinctively I knew she could teach me the basics of survival and what I learned from this astute woman stayed with me throughout my lifetime. At seventy-six, her face was cherubic with few lines, a perpetually innocent look and eyes that sparkled with mischief. We put Buttercup's lid down, packed a lunch, stashed her bottle of gin in a carpetbag, then headed for the Cavalier Hotel on the oceanfront where she had a cabana. After carefully marking the bottle, she gave it to the waiter in a tuxedo.

"Charlie, I've marked the bottle, so be a good boy. We'll have two Singapore Slings. Go light on the little lady's – she's just learning."

I certainly was.

Charlie appeared with the two Singapore Slings and served us as we sat in the cabana on the beach. Iowa had nothing like this. I settled in, feeling right at home as we sipped the afternoon away, while Chintzy taught me the rudiments of a Navy wife's life. The longer she talked, the more I sipped and learned the meaning of Dutch courage. Driving home was my first experience with double lines where there weren't any.

The cockroach appeared from time to time, always in the kitchen sink. I simply waited for him to leave, scrubbed out the sink, then washed my dishes. Knowing little or nothing about what to do with a stove, my diet was unhealthy and minimal except when Chintzy decided I needed proper nourishment.

I was reading *The Pickwick Papers* in the wicker porch chair as Chintzy, in a floppy hat and nurse's shoes, climbed the long flight of steps, puffing with each one. She presented me with a Mason jar full of figs in brown syrup.

"They're off my tree and between saving them from the neighbor and the squirrels, I've had a busy time getting enough to put in a jar." She raised the jar to study its color.

I had heard the shotgun several times and wondered if the neighbor had a new part in her hair. "Chintzy, they look wonderful. I can't wait to try them."

"Go easy on them. You know what figs can do."

I didn't but couldn't imagine they would be anything but nutritious. The next morning, I ladled them into a bowl with the syrup, poured the cream off the top of the milk bottle over them and demolished the whole thing. They not only tasted good, they warmed me. All over.

I slept that day, that night and the next morning until eleven and wakened with my very first hangover. Chintzy had brandied her figs.

He was home! With twenty-two pages to go in *Pickwick*, I glanced up at the car slowing down in front of our house. It stopped and the tall man with dark hair, amber eyes and a slightly rumpled uniform, climbed out. I dropped my book, raced down the front steps, only to miss the next to the last one and land on my knees on the waffled metal foot scraper at the bottom, greeting my warrior with bleeding knees. The car was full of naval officers who simply laughed, shook their heads and probably hoped for an equally enthusiastic greeting from their own wives.

Neither of us noticed my bloody knees until much later.

Patricia Linder

CHAPTER FOUR

1950

As they said in my college course 'Marriage and the Family', I was with child. Of course I was. He was twenty-four, I was twenty - three and we had waited five years to begin our family. His career would always take precedence over my best-laid plans. I was just happy this one slipped through.

We were to report to Pensacola, Florida for flight training. During his years as a Midshipman at the Naval Academy, Jim made the choice to become a naval aviator.

Brows knit, he had said, "You know, I might consider submarines. Some of my friends are leaning that way."

I flapped my hands, shook my head and emphatically said, "NO. I do not want my husband living like a sardine in a can. Besides, it's underwater and I can't swim."

It worked. Not because of my histrionics – he really wanted to fly.

In Pensacola, we moved into a swampy little subdivision next to the dog race- track. It was all any of the Navy families could afford. Pensacola can best be described as hotter than the hinges of hell with humidity to match. Our apartment sported throughout, a wainscoat of mildew three feet high. It was a gray green color, smelled of wet earth and old things and prompted me to place all furniture against the walls in an effort to hide it. .

In the broom closet -sized kitchen was a four burner stove. It measured twenty-two inches square. Jim had thoughtfully provided me with a large iron skillet that took two hands to lift and needed two burners to sit on.

He left with his fellow pilots for flight training classes one scorching September morning. It was my day for Buttercup, my first Wives' Club luncheon and a stop at the butcher shop for a piece of liver. Mother's liver and onions had always been one of my father's favorites but I was vague on what she did with it. .

Near the time the men were due home for the day, I peeled off my summer suit, wrapped an apron around my middle and in my slip, began the battle of the skillet. You have a pan, you have a burner – you get it hot. As Jim was unwinding himself from the back seat of the car pool, I threw the liver in the pan.

It sat for just a moment, then shot skyward and fell to the floor beside the stove where it lay, dark red and quivering.

No one had told me to remove the membrane. As far as I was concerned, it was still alive. I leaped over the liver and shot out the front door with meat fork in hand.

Jim took one look at me, standing on the lawn in my slip. "What's going on here?"

With the car poolers slowly driving by, I established myself as that Navy wife who cooks in her slip and greets her husband with a meat fork.

A good percentage of us were pregnant, thanks to a party celebrating the beginning of flight training. We were all due to deliver about the same time. One close friend, because of a doctor's negligence, lost her baby in the early part of her ninth month. When I recovered from the shock, I decided not to take the chance of losing mine. Since Jim's orders were cut for Corpus Christi, Texas where he would eventually earn his wings, I was adamant about leaving Pensacola. We found one airline that would take me, despite my appearance of an impending emergency. With friends of my family offering to take me in, I flew on to Corpus alone. Jim would follow in a few weeks, when flight training was finished.

I was twenty-one days away from delivery.

Iune in Corpus Christi was hotter than June in Pensacola. I had to learn the bus schedule, check in at the hospital, find a new doctor, and locate a place to live – in that order. I was now fourteen days away from adding to our family.

The naval hospital OB ward was at the end of a concrete runway that radiated heat. I knew my hair would have to go. It was too hot to have anything on me that didn't have to be. As the hair drifted to the floor, I thought of the word, 'sacrifice' that my mother so often used when discussing the raising of children. With my beach-ball shape and a 'poodle cut', popular in the early fifties, I looked like a fat clown as I knocked on doors and pressed doorbells.

I found a duplex with weeds to the waist in the back yard. It was furnished in early nothing but close to the Naval Base. Jim arrived, we bought a fan, Mother flew in and I delivered. That was probably my most important early lesson – the value of timing.

Jim was a thoughtful father-to-be.   He made a majestic entrance into the labor room, shoulders squared and confident. "Hello, old girl. I've just come to wish you luck and bring you something to read.   It shouldn't be much longer, now." How did *he* know? The book was *Eisenhower's Crusade in Europe* and propped on my beach ball belly, it was about the same size.

The doctor looked astonished.   "I'm really impressed, Mrs. Linder. Most of the labor room mothers read comic books or *Ladies Home Journal.*"

I was impressed that he knew my name. "Actually doctor, due to pains that belong in a medieval torture chamber, I am getting very little out of Mr. Eisenhower's '*Crusade*'."

He smiled benignly, patted the beach ball and left me to my agony.

Saddleblock anasthetic shots are given in the back near the spine. Besides numbing you from the waist down, it allows you to count the tiles on the delivery room ceiling and help when called upon. After they were issued to the six expecting mothers in the room, one by one, we were rolled into the operating room for assembly line delivery. I was lucky. When they wakened me the next morning to tell me to go to the nursery to pick up my baby – which I did – the girl next to me could not move her legs. The saddleblock, incorrectly administered, had hit a nerve. She was paralyzed from the waist down.

I marveled at the perfection of my first girl child. The heat was over one hundred degrees with no air conditioning and the runway operating at top speed. Mother, Jamey and I ducked each time a plane roared over the bed.

It was spartan. It was hard. My featherbed life as a child had not prepared me for the harsh realities of Navy life. Making my bed the morning after Jamey was born, I watched the girl with the paralyzed legs hold her new baby with nothing but hope in her eyes. A firm resolve to survive began to form in my mind.

We made our own beds, fetched our babies from the nursery, and took care of them as well as ourselves. Jamey was healthy with fingers and toes in place. I knew if I could just get home and away from the thundering roar of planes in takeoff, I would rock our girl in front of the fan and heal in body and soul. I might even read a page or two from Mr. Eisenhower's book – which by the way, was never read, but stayed with us in our travels for thirty years.

Jim's cool deserted him in the grocery store. I was astonished at his savoire faire over the whole matter of first-time fatherhood until he introduced my mother as his wife and me as his mother-in-law to a squadron friend. Apparently, he was wound tighter than either of us knew.

Two days after Mother left for Iowa, he came home late one afternoon with a live chicken.

"Brought you something, dear." A kiss on the cheek.

"I can see that. It's a live chicken. Are we going into business? If so, we'll need two."

"No, of course not. It's for dinner."

"It's joining us for dinner? Do I set an extra place?'

"No. You cook it."

"No, I don't."

'"My sister would. She used to cook chickens at home."

"So send it to your sister – dear."

Kiss on the cheek.

CHAPTER FIVE

1951

To fully understand a Naval Aviator is a contradiction in itself. There is no such thing. Other aviators' wives might say at this point, "Baloney". But we all know that only through sainthood, can a Navy wife ever really know the man she lives with. These men are a complicated breed, trained at an early age to have complete faith in their own abilities. They are often called cocky, arrogant, egotistical, hard and without mercy. They are taught to lead under any circumstance – to have the courage of their convictions and to understand the importance of discipline and the chain of command. They know decisions must be split second and correct or they're dead. There is no such thing as an excuse. They know, whether Ensign or Admiral, they are totally accountable for their actions.

But after a long separation, they are also, tender, exciting and most important – *there*. In the normal span of a man's career, a couple can experience as many as thirty-two 'second honeymoons' and although not written into the Navy Manual, if they live through them, it's one sure way to keep marriages together, despite the long months and years of separations.

As for my husband, the Naval Academy signed, sealed and delivered him to a career in Naval Aviation. That career shaped our lives. For better or for worse, flying was his chosen field. At the root of it all was motivation and being awarded his wings at the beginning of another war, God and Country were on the top of the list of priorities. Wife and children were somewhat further down and as the war progressed, the *necessity for Security* bumped us yet another notch.

In the flush of victory at the end of the big one, the United States, so wrung out with war, chose to stand down. Nobody wanted to think about it anymore. The military was disassembled as weary men ran for home and family. America used the monies so long designated for defense buildup, to reward the men who had fought for their country, turning their attention from weapons to plows. There was a collective sigh of relief and the firm conviction it wouldn't happen again.

But it did.

A mere five years later, in 1950,we were once again at war but the American public said, "Forget it. We've had enough." Thus, the Korean conflict – always to be known as 'The Forgotten War', began as North Korea invaded South Korea and General Douglas MacArthur was given orders by President Harry Truman to engage the enemy.

Jim chose jets. From Corpus Christi, we returned to Pensacola for the further training that would allow him to fly faster than the speed of sound -- off a carrier deck – at night – in the middle of high seas, only to return again under worse conditions.

I concentrated on baby formulas, cloth diapers that required washing and new motherhood, trying not to think about it. Throw in a war and it was the perfect recipe for a bad case of nerves.

He was quiet when he came home after a day of flight training. The schedule had been more than demanding and I thought he was just tired from that and the heat.

He sat with shoulders slumped. "Remember Kelly?"

"The big Irishman? Of course I remember him. When I last saw him, he mentioned he was the hottest pilot in the class – maybe even in the Navy. He also said that his Emmelmans were perfect, but his Chandelles were superb! Are they teaching you guys 'macho' along with flying?"

The twisting and turning of the Emmelman flight maneuver and the gut-wrenching stalls of a Chandelle were big time flying for new pilots.

With his elbows on his knees, Jim stared at his hands. "He soloed today."

"And....."

"He bought the farm." A quaint little phrase that means his days on earth had just ended.

The big Irishman named Kelly so sure of his expertise and daring, didn't have the wisdom of fear.

It was a hard lesson for his classmates, but one they never forgot. Nor did I. It could have been Jim. A knot of fear took root in the back of my mind, there to fester and grow for the next thirty years. Thank God we were young. The euphoria of a new marriage and a new child, had allowed me the luxury of confidence. Never again would that confidence be that strong. My blooding ground was still ahead. The future stretched like a taut rubber band. Knowing we had the 'bomb' gave little comfort, for like the plague, that monster would spread to other countries with the money and expertise to produce it.

Our generation's motto was, 'Live today, for tomorrow, you may die'. Any wonder?

Yet, the baby had to be diapered, husband wanted his dinner on time, and the first experience of 'playing house' for real, charmed me. I did it the only way I knew how – as my mother had. Thus, the menacing threat of the future was tempered by the gentleness of the past.

Jet training completed and with golden wings on his uniform, we made a swift Christmas visit to our parents in Iowa to show them the new baby. They knew we were on orders to San Diego and that meant an aircraft carrier, headed west.

West was war.

Silently, I blessed them for not asking the many questions that must have crowded their thoughts. We could only guess what was ahead.

When little Buttercup was traded for a big, second -hand Buick, a small piece of my heart went with her. We looked quite grand, fully loaded with baby gear, suitcases and 'little things' for our first home. I was excited to be making my maiden trip West.

The worst winter on record set in and I learned how much more frightened a woman can be when she's holding her first born, with the car sliding sideways down a hill of ice. But we came to a complete halt in Amarillo, Texas when a blizzard prevented Jim from seeing the hood ornament on the car. Through a solid wall of white, we were able to make out the colors of a neon sign.   Hoping it said 'Motel', we stopped for the night. The room was tiny with a cracked, linoleum floor and a bare light bulb dangling from the ceiling. A kerosene stove was the only warmth and the bathroom was so bad, I made a concentrated effort to forget it. At the Mexican restaurant next door, I heated Jamey's formula in a kitchen moving with roaches. It was New Year's Eve.

Putting our girl between us for warmth, we spent a miserable night under a threadbare blanket. Someone cared, for the storm ended just before dawn. On January first 1951, we left without a backward glance.

San Diego, 1951

"Does it cry?"

We stood on the out side of the screen door, looking like Girl Scouts, selling cookies, only the cookie I held was our baby. Inside, a stocky woman with short hair, steely eyes, and a mustache on her upper lip peered at us belligerently. I wondered if 'she' was a man in a dress.

"It" was Jamey.   As the woman knew, we were desperate for a place to stay. Due to the military buildup, all the motels were filled, so we had cruised the streets, looking for moving vans that might mean a vacancy. We slept in the car that night. Morning found us on a doorstep, after watching the unfriendly one post a *For Rent* sign on the front lawn.

Following Amarillo, we had streaked for California. Something happens to a naval officer when he's on orders. The route becomes the shortest distance between two points and it's 600 to 700 miles a day, or bust. It might have something to do with the abiding fear of being AWOL. Whatever –I hung diapers out the car window to dry in Arizona, saw Bryce National Canyon by flashlight and arrived in Coronado, California glassy-eyed.

After an immediate check-in with the Navy, Jim found he would be stationed on Coronado, North Island, a ferryboat ride away from San Diego for advanced training in operational deployment – or in wives' words, 'get ready to go to war'. We would stay for three months before moving to the next phase – a fighter squadron at another base.

"Does it cry?"

I had been too tired and too stunned to make a coherent statement about anything.

But Jim said, "No ma'am -- hardly ever cries and my wife always takes her out in the stroller if she does."

It occurred to me my work was cut out for me. I would be spending a lot of my time on the streets of Coronado. But with the hazy view of a spacious, airy first floor apartment over the dragon lady's shoulder. I would have promised her anything short of my first born's soul. A deal was struck and we unpacked the car.

'It' didn't make a sound.

Unlike Norfolk, Virginia with its signs on the front lawns that read, 'Sailors and dogs, KEEP OFF THE GRASS', Coronado was pragmatic about the fast influx of Navy families. The Naval Base with its tight security and eight- foot chain link fences, gave the touch of menace to the otherwise idyllic scene.

We stayed for three months, and rain or shine, when Jamey tuned up – as babies will – I walked the streets, learning the town.

But our paradise was short lived. Jim was sent to the Miramar Naval Air Station, making it necessary to move into Wherry Housing in San Diego – government provided, little more than a tenement and with a next-door neighbor who had active tuberculosis. Her husband was at sea, so after two emergency trips to Balboa hospital when she hemorrhaged, I knew helping her would only endanger my own family. We made the decision to buy our first house.

Jim transitioned into the plane he would be flying in Korea -- the F-9F Panther jet, a slim, sleek looking plane with fuel pods at the end of each wing, and a far cry from the slow but sure SNJ propeller plane he had first trained in. The squadron was an entity unto itself-- a tight little island. The civilian population preferred not to be reminded we were at war, so we hunkered down, developed our own shorthand language, complete with Navy acronyms and concentrated on our children.

My protective shell began to form.

Our first brush with the chain of command came on a Sunday morning as we lounged in our pajamas, reading the paper. Jamey needed a diaper change, but I was too relaxed in our new home on the mountain -top to worry about it for another fifteen minutes. Out of the corner of my eye, I noticed a car stopping at our curb. Like a snake watching a mongoose, I saw Jim's Commanding Officer, accompanied by his white-gloved wife, step out and head up our driveway.

There had been no advance notice.

"My God, Jim. It's your CO and his wife. Put on your pants."

The papers went under the couch, my robe tail hit the flat wood surfaces in the room as I scooped up Jamey and fled for the bedroom to change. That was the day I learned how to clean house in under ten seconds. It would serve me well for the next twenty-nine years, as would the two words that lodged in the back of my mind after that sleepy, happy Sunday.

On guard.

CHAPTER SIX

To fully understand a Navy wife, you need to be one. We are indeed, a different breed of cat. Our backgrounds vary in location, education and affluence – or lack of. We come into a highly structured way of life, assuming we can bend it to meet our own needs. The first brick wall is learning we can't. It's serious business, what our husbands do and that rubs off on home life. We have 'NO NEED TO KNOW', a bit of Pentagonese designed to drive wives crazy, surpassed only by 'he will be gone indefinitely'. Without a sense of humor, a Navy wife will not last. She will, in Navy terms, be dead in the water.

The greatest education she will ever receive is the one about herself. None of us, of course, knows that in the beginning. Love for the man we married, pride in what he does for a living and hope for an exciting, manageable future starts us off. What we do with that is strictly up to us. Some make it, some don't.

The winnowing- out begins with a combat cruise. After the men leave on an eight- month deployment to a destination thousands of miles away with the possibility of being shot out of the sky by the enemy, occasionally a young wife will say, "I can't do this. I'm going home to Mother." It's a recurring nightmare for the rest of us. But the answer to that is to look at Susie, Jane or Muriel, who choose to remain and say, "If she can do it, so can I." After all, our husbands are already heroes, if only in our own eyes and no hero needs a wimp for a wife. Strong words – but it took strong words to keep us nailed to our responsibilities

Our first house perched near the top of a mountain east of San Diego. Measuring 1000 square feet at a cost of $12,000, built on rock fill but with a kitchen window that looked out on the Laguna Mountains, I knew my first home had charm and better yet, was mine to play with. It did not have a front or back yard. The potential was there, but so were the rocks.

The ship, on a wartime basis was due to sail in a scant two months. Being a lowly Ensign, Jim's shipmates saw more of him than I did. On Christmas Eve 1951,because he had the duty, Jamey and I boarded the carrier, Phillipine Sea to spend the afternoon and evening with him. A movie was provided on the hanger deck for the children, there to be with their fathers on such an important night. Jamey stood in the aisle on her eighteen-month-old legs that still wobbled a bit when she was tired. Entranced with the movie, she was determined not to miss a moment of it.

The carrier began to rock from side to side. Although tied up, the huge ship bumped and slammed against the pier. It was an earthquake – a heavy one. Jamey's baby legs gave out as she landed flat on her diaper-padded ruffled rear. The result was a damage control assessment of the ship and a hurried evacuation of the visiting families.

Soon after, with a full complement of planes and over five thousand men, the U.S.S.Phillipine Sea slowly moved out of the harbor, thick with skimming sail boats and fishing trawlers. Tugs were snuggled up to its massive sides, guiding it through the difficult waters to the mouth of the harbor where the Pacific Ocean began. Holding Jamey, I stood on the dock for our first goodbye. We watched until it was just a speck in the distance. .

My thoughts centered on the man who had held us both for the short time allowed, then pushed us gently toward the gangway. He was torn – I knew that. He was leaving his family for eight months. We were still newly-weds, our baby was new, the house was new and the car, almost new. Earthquakes happened. He was putting his entire worldly goods in the hands of a klutz who falls down stairs. I'm sure there was apprehension in his mind.

"I'll send money home every time I'm paid on the ship, but on Ensign's pay, there will only be enough to cover the house payment, the utilities and food."

Three hundred dollars a month, with a little out for his own needs was mine to manage. It didn't look much greater than the $64 we started out with after our wedding. But I knew where he was going and what awaited him at the other end. I vowed to make it work. It was the eight months without him that overshadowed any financial problems. The simple act of going to bed alone, night after night, not knowing if he was alive or dead, drove me to the closet to lean against his sport coats and try to remember his touch or the sound of his voice. Still too new to the life, I couldn't imagine surviving the next eight months.

He knew what waited for him too, and that knowledge alone, caused the sadness of parting to move over for the sparkle of his first 'operational' tour of duty. As the young pilots trained, they were heard to say, "You're a fighter or a lover – you can't be both." It must have had something to do with concentration. But like little boys, they wanted their cake and eat it, too. Today, they were fighters and the adrenaline was up. The months of training precluded any thoughts of wife and family. Now that training would finally pay off with hypotheticals becoming realities. Using their expertise, they would have the chance to prove themselves in battle. I doubt if any of them thought about 'the enemy' at that moment. The world of men, their planes waiting for them on the flight deck and hangar bays, was forming as a solid weapon of war and they were excited and proud to be a part of it.

"Jamey, we girls have our work cut out for us."

We sat on the front steps, my daughter and I, surveying our world. The perfect blue of a San Diego sky beckoned us to begin.

"Punkin', there must be ten million rocks out there."

"I know't, Mommy."

"What are we going to do about it, small girl?'

She handed me the screwdriver that rested on the step between us. "Dig, Mommy." She was very much, her father's child.

We dug for days. The southwest corner of the yard became our rock pile. A neighbor thoughtfully loaned me his wheelbarrow (but not his muscles).

"Jamey girl, what do you think about planting some flowers for a change?"

"I think just fine."

"Any druthers on what kind?"

She cocked her head with this big decision. "I think red."

"You bet'cha. Let's go find a nursery."

Eighty -two red and white carnation plants went into the cinder block planter that wrapped around the front and side of our house. Following the instructions page by page, from 'Putting in a Lawn in Southern California', I spread dirt, fertilized with cow manure from a nearby farm and rented a lawn roller.

Filled with water, it was like pushing Hoover Dam.

The book said, 'Plant a grain crop first." I planted wheat and when it was high enough to bend in the wind like an Iowa wheat field, I sat down on the porch steps and cried from sheer homesickness. But there was the Kentucky Blue Grass to be sowed into the wheat. With the fascinated neighbors watching every move, I borrowed a scythe from the manure farmer, scythed down the wheat and stopped traffic as people drove by to watch this modern day peasant clear her field.

Mother and Dad arrived for a month-long visit and the three of us put in the back yard and laid two patios. They left exhausted and stunned that their daughter's life was one of hard labor.

The day came when our small towheaded child and I sat on our front steps, looking at the perfect emerald green lawn and the eighty-two fragrant carnations. Our applauding neighbors and the slowly passing cars told us we were a legend in our own time.

When Jim's eight-month tour of combat duty was completed, Jamey and I met the great, gray, tired ship. Emotion runs high when the gangway is lowered into place and the wives and children are allowed aboard. The men have lined the rails, looking for a wife or a girlfriend. When they spot their chosen one, eyes lock and the moving, anxious crowd fades away. Even from afar, silent messages fly across the distance, then as the families slowly file aboard, arms reach out and pluck them away for moments of unrestrained emotion. Few words are spoken. Although the crowd grows, it's the quiet that one remembers.

As we drove up our mountain, holding tightly to each other, the most beautiful lawn in the world came into view. I heard him draw in his breath with pleasure. Every swipe of the scythe had been worth it.

CHAPTER SEVEN

1950

The Forgotten War began six days before our daughter was born. June 25[th,] 1950 It launched a new kind of war, perhaps in deference to the American public that wanted nothing to do with it. The term 'limited war' was coined and as time would prove, it was a sure recipe for defeat. A chosen few would fight in Korea, but it was the wrong war and the wrong time. In thirty-seven months, 25,000 Americans would die there. 8,000 would be missing or prisoners and never heard of again. Compared to the nearly 34,000 who would give up their lives over a ten year period in Viet Nam, it was a bona fide conflict. But the American media had other fish to fry. Senator Joe McCarthy was striking down anyone with a flushed face –'Red is Communist', the country was working its way through a recession, the movies cranked out two- hour sagas of war about Pearl Harbor, Anzio, the Bulge, Okinawa – any battle that raged during the first half of the Forties and if you attended, that was your patriotic charge for the day. Just don't bother us about the one that's going on now.

They were still doing it like they had in the big one. When a man was lost in battle, be he dead, missing or a prisoner of war, his wife received a letter from the U.S. government, informing her of the loss of her husband. Cut and dried. The ball was now in her court. The system would improve for the next war, but in Korea, if you were in the Prisoner of War category, you became a statistic, destined to remain in whatever slave labor camp they put you for the rest of your life.

Jim didn't tell me these things, but I listened to the conversations at squadron parties. We knew of other wives who had received The Letter, and within the Navy community, Korea was very much a war. What was happening there was no different from any other conflict. We knew where the 38th parallel was. When it became apparent that the Chinese Communists had sent 800,000 troops and Soviet tanks to join forces with the North Koreans, the heat escalated. More strikes were flown off the carriers – sometimes two and three a day for many of the pilots.

Being an Ensign – the lowest rung on the Officer ladder, Jim became a 'Tailend Charlie'. He flew the combat strikes at the back of the squadron formation. It would take the North Koreans time to pinpoint the attacking planes and often, when the enemy made their anti-aircraft 'fix', the squadron was safely past. Except for the Charlies. Being new at the game of war and less experienced than the others they were expendable. So I learned these things, stored them in my memory and played at living a normal, happy life. Don't make waves.

It worked for nine months until Jim mentioned he was to return to Korea. In June of 1953, Jamey and I once again stood on the dock, watching as the aircraft carrier, Kearsarge, sailed away. I was five months away from the birth of our second child. The pretty house with its perfect lawn and the eighty-two carnations, was sold. Jim had lived in it less than a year and without a set of orders, we decided to pack up and store our worldly goods. I had the train tickets to Iowa in my purse. .

It was mutually agreed I would return to my parents to have our baby. From a practical standpoint, should Jim be killed, I would be in the right place. With the house sold, our bridges were burnt.

He went West. I went East.

My country slipped by me as Jamey napped and I looked at the great expanses of land so varied in climate and topography. How easy it had always been to take it for granted. But I was wiser now, and knew that everything had its price. During World War II, the cushion of youth, protection and comfort had kept its ugliness at bay. Now, I was a participant with one small life and another one soon, who would depend on me for everything.

Iowa, 1953

I was relieved to be back in the warm arms of family and friends. Being five months pregnant, a husband who was somewhere – nobody really knew where and neither did I at that point, I sensed I was somewhat of a freak to my little town. My conversations were nebulous, generalized and I wore the protective armor of a military wife in time of peace. Peace – if they only knew. Tunnel vision was rampant and I was the reminder of what they were determined to forget. Yet, because of the innate kindness of the native Midwesterner, it was a good summer. My baby was due in October, but it would be late February before Jim met his son. In the meantime, we kept busy.

The month before school began, the High School Band practiced on our street and with my father standing by, Jamey, with hair that went every-which-way, hunkered down at the foot of the driveway and solemnly watched the tramping feet of reluctant students, still mesmerized by a lazy summer. The whistles blew, the batons flashed and as she squatted with clasped hands and watched the formations change, her little rump kept time to the beat of the bass drum.

Three days a week for two months, I walked her to a play-school at the top of our hill. On the Monday after Labor Day, it would become a preschool and she was already enrolled.

The autumn days were perfect as only Iowa can provide. The air was soft, but with the touch of coolness to come. It was a time for waiting. I knew that soon, Jamey would begin what she called 'my school' and to her, it was the beginning of the big time. To me, it meant the first letting go. I wasn't ready for it and wondered if I would ever be. The Arabic poet, Kahlil Gibran had said that the child was the arrow, the parent the bow, and there must come the time for the arrow to fly. Mr. Gibran had never been the *mother* of a three - year -old. I wanted that little arrow in my quiver for a very long time, but she had ideas of her own.

By September, and in every sense of the word, I was once again, great with child. A box arrived from the Far East and to my astonishment, I found my husband had sent me a mink stole. Wrapping its deep brown silkiness around my shoulders and crossing it in front over my soon-to-be-born son, I looked like a mink expecting a large litter. No matter. He had remembered my birthday from thousands of miles away, saved the money and made the time and effort to purchase something that would make me feel cherished. I could only imagine the logistics involved and feeling like a woman again, instead of a fat mother, I let the loneliness and fear for him take over. The discipline of strength deserted me and this girl had a real good cry.

Warren Rogers was the editor of the Mt. Pleasant Daily News. I had worked in the clattering, ink-stained offices as a summer job teenager and found it exciting, taking the news over the telephone, then watching the experts transform it into a newspaper that had to be out and on the doorsteps by five o'clock in the evening. Our families were friends and our houses were next door to each other. Warren called me late one morning and after our mutual greetings, said, "Patti, I'm calling to apologize to you. I have just finished reading the book, *The Bridges of Toko Ri'* and I didn't know."

I was stunned and delighted. With his words, he validated our way of life. The book spoke of a Navy pilot, shot down by enemy fire, huddled in a ditch, waiting to be taken prisoner or shot by the enemy. The man's thoughts centered on the complete indifference of the American public to the war in Korea.

"Thank you, Warren. I've been cautioned not to read it until Jim returns. Is that good advice?"

"As your long-time friend, take that advice. But Patti, when you do read it, remember my apology. We must seem very uncaring to you."

"I've never in all my years, known you to be uncaring, Warren. It's Jim's choice to be where he is and my choice to support him in what he does." I felt a jolt of pride in being able to say that.

Had I known that one of Jim's choices was to be on the ground in Korea on Pork Chop Hill with the Infantry, crouched in a foxhole while the mortar fire exploded all around him, I might have qualified that statement.

He had flown reconnaissance flights over the other carriers off the coast, as a matter of protection for the fleet. Dull duty. When the call came for volunteers to fly in light planes over Korea with the intent of spotting possible target areas for the ground forces, Jim and three other pilots held up their hands. Once in Korea, he determined it would be beneficial to his fellow pilots to know how they did it on the ground. The Army had long ago made public its evaluation of Navy pilots who breezed around in the overhead, only to return to their ship where a hot meal and clean sheets awaited them.

Apparently that stung, for here was Jim now, in the worst possible place in Korea, face to face with the enemy, only a few hundred yards away and vowing never to volunteer for anything again. His job was to observe the North Korean/Chinese positions and our mortar positions for close air support. Unarmed, but with a camera slung over his shoulder, he took pictures of the battle. When the pictures were developed, they clearly showed the mushroom of concussion from bomb bursts a few yards away.

Men were dying around him in the snow and rain. He was pinned down in a foxhole but during a break in the fighting, a Jeep and driver arrived at the company installation nearby and Jim was told to get to the Jeep and get out of there. As he made a run for it, enemy mortar fragments hit and badly wounded the driver. Another man took his place. They were able to escape the bombings, but the intensity of the battle drove soldiers and Marines alike into culverts or drainpipes under the road.

Pork Chop Hill was a protracted battle that raged for several weeks, but the information Jim and the other three pilots took back to the Squadron proved invaluable as the war wore on.

Had I known. But I was not to learn of this particular episode until many months later after I had completed reading *The Bridges of Toko Ri..* By then, I could only be very proud of what he had done, with the caveat of wondering if he thought of his family on these chosen adventures. I was still new to the game.

Patricia Linder

CHAPTER EIGHT

1953

It was the kind of Iowa homecoming they make movies about. The warrior, returning from the wars was surrounded by parents and in-laws, his happy wife, adoring little daughter and a brand new son who resembled Winston Churchill more than his father. There was laughter and tears, gifts for everybody and the wonder a man feels when he sees his son for the first time.

Jim had ten days of leave and although the February weather was cold and snowy, the fires were kept burning in the fireplace and people dropped in for hot coffee and Mother's angel food cake. We visited back and forth between the two sets of parents, Jamey resplendent in her authentic Japanese kimono with its little obi and Jeffrey soundly asleep as he was passed from arms to arms. It was a happy time. For all of us, the war was over and Jim would not have to do it again.

How naïve.

My husband looked different. There were lines on his face I had never noticed before. His eyes had a hooded look as though he was seeing something we couldn't. Our moments alone together were still sweet with passion, but the abandon of a young marriage was gone, replaced by a distracted gentleness. I felt he had grown up and away from us. His life was so different from ours, I wondered if we would ever recapture the easy love we had felt for each other for so long.

One more fear to join the others that had settled in the back of my thoughts.

Reluctantly, we said our goodbyes and flew to San Diego for new orders to Pensacola and the Training Command. He would be a flight instructor and having already lived there twice, I was looking forward to familiar territory. The Buick came out of storage and because there was a wait of three or four months before the orders were executed, we moved once again into temporary Wherry housing. We were on the ground floor and the little boy upstairs had his first pair of roller skates.

As the movers began the job of placing the furniture for a three-bedroom house into a two- bedroom apartment half the size of our home on the mountain, Jim appeared at the front door with papers in his hand and a cautious look on his face.

He almost ducked his head when he said, "Patti, this is a new set of orders that just came in. We're to go to Willow Grove, Pennsylvania instead of Pensacola. It's Shore Duty."

The movers and I were rooted to the spot. "Jim, what are you talking about? You have orders to Pensacola in three months."

"I did, but I don't any more."

I looked at the chaos of furniture and boxes. "There's no water in Pennsylvania. You're in the Navy. Don't you need water for that?"

"It's Shore Duty, honey. Maybe even three years of it."

"In one place?"

"It's just north of Philadelphia...out in the country. I'll be training Reserves. I'll be home every night for dinner."

He almost lost me on that last one.

In front of Jim and the movers, I sat down on the floor and counted on my fingers.

"Including this one, we've had ten address changes in three and a half years."

The little boy upstairs strapped on his skates and began his training for the Olympics. Jeffrey tuned up in his car bed in the second bedroom. We all looked at each other. Then one of the movers shrugged, picked up the last carton he had just dropped on the floor and trudged out to the truck.

Pennsylvania, here we come.

For the five days it took us to drive to the East Coast, we talked. While still in the squadron, he preferred not to discuss his work. 'Security' would always be an ominous presence between us. Conversations could ripple along and then suddenly cease.

I understood the reasons, but the war was over for us and I felt entitled to some enlightenment about how he had spent those sixteen months out of our three and a half years of marriage. It would be my reward for being a good Navy wife who did everything she was supposed to, though some of it through gritted teeth.

I was curious about everything – the ship, the planes, the strikes and Korea, itself.

Jim's long fingers drummed on the steering wheel. "Remember, I was new to combat when I first joined the ship. Because of that, I flew a lot of patrols over the fleet when it was off the coast of Korea."

Knowing him, I could imagine his frustration. The drumming fingers made his point. "All our flights were off the carrier and those carriers weren't made for jets. They used prop planes during World War II , but instead of coming in for a landing at 90 knots, in jets we came in at 125 knots. With a bunch of planes parked at the far end of the flight deck, it was pretty hairy." I couldn't take my eyes off his hands. They clenched and I realized he was reliving one of those 'hairy' landings.

"What happened if you couldn't stop in time?" As if I didn't know.

"Well, all carriers have a number of steel cables stretching across their flight decks. During landing, the tailhook on the plane catches one of these 'wires' and stops the plane in about 300 feet."

"What if it doesn't?" I stopped watching his hands and listened very carefully. This was stuff I needed to know.

"If that failed, the emergency system kicked in. Additional steel cables and heavy nylon straps, would act as a barricade to stop the aircraft before it crashed into parked planes near the bow of the ship"

I was getting a graphic picture of this in my mind and it wasn't a pretty one.

He went on. "There was one small problem. The barricade cables were heavy and sat up a ways off the deck and occasionally, they'd peel off your landing gear." He checked the rear-view mirror for oncoming traffic.

"So, if your tailhook didn't hook the arresting gear, and the barricade cables took off your landing gear, you slid into the parked planes at the end of the deck. Right?"

"Right."

I really didn't want to know much more of this.

The jets they flew had been built in the five- year span of time between WWII and Korea when military aircraft production had been reduced by thirty percent. Aviation had gone from propeller planes to jets very quickly and without the funds they needed.

Jim continued. "They didn't really have time to iron out all the glitches before putting the planes back into combat and sometimes things didn't work. Our navigational systems were not good enough for the type plane we flew and those carrier decks were just too short."

I was grateful I hadn't known this before the cruise.

"Did they know that, when you were doing carrier qualification flights?"

During his training years, the pilots did 'care quals', their name for touch and go landings and takeoffs on land-based airfields in preparation for carrier flight decks.

Jim shook his head. "We assumed the Navy knew about the problem. There wasn't much they could do about it, anyway." He paused as he passed a semi. "The carriers left over from World War II are all we have and not enough defense money to make any changes on them for this war. They didn't expect another one so soon. Radar was pretty inadequate, too. But that's it, and until somebody comes up with a better way, we're stuck with it. One thing I know now for a fact is, you don't assume a thing –not a damned thing."

"I know you flew strikes over North Korea from what the other wives told me. Can you talk about your targets, now that it's over?"

"Mostly bridges and dams. We did some pretty heavy -duty stuff on the Chosin Reservoir."

It was a familiar name that had actually made it into the newspaper.

"We flew close air support with the Air Force over front lines when they needed us, but if you asked them, they would probably deny we were ever there."

That's called 'interservice rivalry' and it will never go away.

Jeff stirred, I checked my watch and plugged the bottle warmer into the cigarette lighter. Jamey was curled around her old yellow blanket with her Japanese doll against her cheek.

"What's Korea like?"

"Bitter cold, scorching hot, rain, snow. Miserable. I'll give those ground troops and Marines credit. They had a dirty job and I guess it's not too different from the way the Japanese fought in World War II. Lots of guerilla tactics. The country itself is very mountainous, rice paddies, lots of cover for snipers and enemy ground troops. Oh, and we saw Russian Migs when we were out on strikes."

"*Russian Migs?* Were the Russians flying them? I knew about the Chinese getting into the act, but was Russia there, too?"

"We couldn't tell who was flying them, but they were jets and probably hadn't been around any longer than ours had. A lot of the ordinance; bombs, guns, tanks – that kind of thing, came from Russia, so we assumed they were more involved than they let on." Years later, we would find out that many American Prisoners of War were sent from North Korea to Russia to spend the rest of their lives in Siberian forced labor camps.

"Thank God it's over and you don't have to go back." Even as I spoke, a shiver of premonition went through me.

The lines deepened in his face. "It's not over, Patti. I don't know if it will ever be over. These are Orientals with the patience they're famous for and if, by some miracle we win this one, sometime they'll come after us again."

The thought of more combat cruise left me speechless. Was this to be the pattern of our lives? Was war our common denominator? I knew it was what Jim had signed on for, but my three -year taste of it had left me knowing I liked none of it. Pride and patriotism stepped aside and the yearning for a normal life, took its place.

Now, how do I deal with this?

As I cradled Jeffrey and gave him his bottle, I let the peacefulness of motherhood edge out the thoughts of war. That would always be a dichotomy in our life together -- the wages of war versus the needs of a family.

Best taken in small doses, I chose not to continue my questions.. As time went on, he would tell me what he felt I should know – nothing more. The battle of Pork Chop Hill was yet to come.

Willow Grove, Pennsylvania provided us with our second home and friends who would last for the rest of our lives. It was a training base for Reserve Navy pilots and Jim was one of their flight instructors. With three years ahead of us, Jamey could begin school and have playmates. I could plan ahead on anything I wanted to. We were a family together with an ongoing war behind us.

But it was not without its moments of sheer terror.

There is a policy in the Navy that should danger come, the planes are taken out of harm's way. Dependents don't argue with policy. One of the worst hurricanes to ever hit the East Coast, plowed into the Philadelphia area and we were in the way on its march into Massachusetts. Of course the planes had to be evacuated.

Jim called from the Base. "Uh, Patti?"

This was my first time around with this particular policy and I walked right into it.

"Hi, dear. I've been securing everything around the house and will start on candles and matches next. There are plenty of canned goods but I'm not sure how to stockpile water. When will you be coming home from the Base?"

"Uh, Patti, listen. I've got to fly a plane to Buffalo, New York in ten minutes and will be there until the storm goes on through and it's safe to bring it back."

"If the storm wasn't so close, that would be funny. Now what time are you coming home?"

One more "Uh, Patti" and I blew. "Are you telling me the kids and I are going to ride out this hurricane by ourselves because of a stupid airplane? Hasn't the Navy heard of women and children first?" From that point on, my anger produced little more than babble and I vaguely heard Jim say,

"Gotta go, Babe. Don't worry, everything will be fine." Gone.

When I cooled down, it occurred to me that Jim was only one of many pilots who would leave wife and kiddies that stormy afternoon. Through gritted teeth, I thought, 'if they can do it, so can we'.

Our house was new with construction going on all around us. I looked across the street at a house in the framing stage and wondered where those boards would go when the hurricane struck. Probably through our picture window.

The electricity went off and the children and I struggled the mattresses up against the big window in the living room. Then with candles, we positioned ourselves in the inner hallway, sleeping on towels and throw rugs. The bathtub was sterilized and filled to the brim with cold water. The hatches were battened down and we held onto each other as things whistled past, banging and slamming against the house. A neighbor crept on his hands and knees to tell me a basement window had blown open. He closed it and hugging the ground, made it back to his own family. It was a long night but our new brick house held fast.

By the following night, the storm had moved on, leaving us with pouring rain and still no electricity. The children and I played King Arthur at Camelot, carrying candles from room to room. Because of the darkness, we hauled the mattresses back onto the beds and fell into exhausted sleep.

In the middle of the night, I heard knocking and scratching on my window-.screen. Looking out, I saw Jim, standing in the downpour, hair plastered to his head. Grabbing a flashlight, I ran to the back door to let him in.

"I thought you were in sunny Buffalo." A small puddle was forming on the kitchen floor and he smelled like jet fuel.

"Was. They let me fly back a few hours ago. Is everything all right here?"

"We haven't had electricity for two days but nothing blew away. I haven't been out to look for damage. The framing across the street isn't there anymore, and I have no idea where the boards went."

"I've got to get out of these clothes and get dry." He looked worn out.

I fell into bed and was just on the edge of sleep, when I heard Jim's shout in the bathroom. Having no lights, he peeled off his wet clothes and stepped into the tub. It was ice cold. My fault. I grinned. I should have remembered to tell him. Now all my good sterilized water was no longer fit to drink and the following two weeks without either electricity or water lasted forever.

CHAPTER NINE

Summer, 1954

The sirens screamed as we careened through Philadelphia traffic, headed for the hospital. Jeffrey lay in his father's arms, his face a mass of blood. I held towels against the wounds to stop the bleeding, but it just kept pumping. A good friend, Bob Anthony, had pushed us into his car, tied a bloody handkerchief to the radio antenna and was now speeding down the freeway. A police car spotted the handkerchief and passed us with lights flashing and sirens at full volume. The patrolman signaled Bob to follow.

The evening was such a happy one. We were with good friends in Willow Grove. A Marine couple had invited us to a pot luck barbecue and the tables full of food reminded me of church socials in Iowa with friends and children milling around. In the busy kitchen that smelled of casseroles in the oven, Jim sat on a straight-backed chair, holding Jeffrey on his lap with his arms around him. Jeff was laughing, his eyes dancing. He loved a good party, even at the age of one and a half. That was his favorite place to be. He held a water glass full of ice cubes in his hands but it slipped from his grasp and fell to the floor. Automatically, Jeff jumped out of his father's arms to go after it and fell face first on the smashed glass.

The rest became a blur, but someone propelled me toward the back door, someone else wrapped his little body in bath towels and handed him to Jim and we found ourselves racing for the hospital.

He was so quiet in Jim's arms, but I did not allow myself any thought but to stop the bleeding. My mind shut down – only my body responded and I tried to automatically do what was necessary. The police car ran the red light, motioning us to follow. There was only silence in the car. Bob was concentrating on driving, Jim was intent on keeping Jeff immobile and I was busy with the towel and handkerchiefs. No one spoke. We each concentrated on our job.

Eternity can be only minutes long. Ours finally ended as the police car swept into the Emergency entrance. We ran. Later, I would recall the professionalism of everyone around us; the quiet swiftness as they took Jeffrey from his father's arms and into an operating room, the soft questions from a nurse with a ruddy complexion and large hands. The smell of the hospital eased the smell of my son's blood and I let the police officer and Jim lead me to waiting chairs across the hall from the OR doors. Bob had parked his car and came hurriedly into the hospital, a frantic look on his face.

There was so much blood on my hands, I could only stare at them. They were sticky. I had to clean them. I walked to the water fountain and held first one hand, then the other under the puny flow of water. Someone guided me to the ladies' room and still with no conscious thought, I mechanically went through the ritual of ridding my hands of my son's blood.

The patrolman left after a few words of good luck and we sat, staring at the door with Jeff behind it. More doctors and extra nurses came. There was a flurry of activity – people moving quickly, seriously, avoiding our questioning eyes.

Four hours later, at midnight, a doctor came through the door. He held our son, wrapped in a hospital baby blanket. Placing Jeff in his father's arms, he wearily rolled his shoulders, then spoke softly to us.

"Your son's going to make it. Because he lost so much blood, we couldn't anesthetize him, so he went through it all, awake. His eyes are all right"

I locked my knees to keep them from buckling.

"His heart stopped twice during the surgery, but everything looks good now."

For four hours, we had listened to Jeffrey's cries that gradually dwindled down to moans as we waited across the hall. Now I knew why.

I studied Jeff's little face. He looked like a baby porcupine with sprouting black stitches that marched across his forehead and his upper lip.

"We stitched from the inside out and there are a lot of them you can't see. I've left them long because he's a baby and they're less likely to pull out. Take him home, now, watch him and call me in the morning." His eyes were kind and compassionate.

In a voice, rough with emotion and relief, Jim said, "You don't think he should stay here overnight?" For the first time, I saw the blood on his shirt.

"No. We've monitored him carefully for the last hour and he's strong and stable. Home would be better for all of you." A wise man, the doctor.

71

Jamey was with Bob's wife, Dottie and eventually, we would have our family back together again at home. I spent the night, sitting on the floor by Jeff's crib, my hand on his arm. Exhausted, he slept deeply and quietly. I awoke to find him sitting up in his crib, tugging on my hand with the words, "Onjuice, Mommy?"

Orange juice it was and as my shaking hand poured it, I could feel the bandage I had laid across my mind, begin to slip. Shock was wearing off, but the discipline learned during the past five years, kept me together.

When Jamey came home, we prepared her for the sight of her brother. She had spent a fearful night, not knowing if he was still alive, but the Anthonys had cared for her with tenderness and kindness.

As we walked down the hallway to his room, Jeff called to his sister..

"Dzammie? I'm in 'ere."

It was quite a reunion. Jamey thought the little porcupine looked pretty awful and told him so. He laughed as much as the prickly stitches would let him then took another sip of his orange juice.

We all began to heal.

It was our luck that the emergency doctor on duty that night was the leading plastic surgeon in all of Philadelphia. There would be scars, but only we who lived through that terrible night, would know they were there.

Two days later as I fixed his lunch, the little porcupine sat on a high kitchen stool, playing a frying pan. It was his guitar and with coonskin cap on sideways, tail over his left ear he serenaded me with "Daveeeey – Davey Crocket."

These were three years of being together as a family. The Navy calls it Shore Duty. It would be twelve years before we had another one of that length.

When your husband is a pilot, there is a phenomenon called 'cross-countries.' It's a form of training. Jim did a lot of training.

"Honey, I have a cross country flight coming up on Friday." – or Tuesday – or Thursday – I lost track. Once, I delivered him to the field at dawn, but instead of hurrying home, I lingered to watch him take off. There is an indescribable feeling to see a sleek, murderous-looking plane streak down a runway knowing that your husband is at the controls. The danger, ever present is confirmation of a life being lived on the edge. I understood his delight in flying, with or without motives, but until that morning, I didn't have the complete picture. As I watched, I saw him emerge from the hanger, tall and lean in his flight suit, dark hair ruffled by the morning breeze and stride toward his plane. Two men followed him. When they stopped by the F-9, bearing Jim's name on its side, they moved forward, handed him his helmet, adjusted the straps, checked his suit then settled him into the waiting Panther Jet. No wonder he liked cross- countries. He was treated like visiting royalty.

I grinned. Obviously, it was up to me to keep him humble.

Knowing he owed me time for myself, Jim passed on a few cross-countries to baby sit the children while I joined the Willow Grove Little Theatre and played Miss Madrigal in Enid Bagnold's *Chalk*

Garden. The theatre would always be in my blood because of previous training and doing that show was like a transfusion. I was good for another ten thousand miles.

The *Philadelphia Enquirer* was spread out on the dining room table. I circled the advertisement with Jamey's magic marker.

George Bernard Shaw's		Rex Harrison
PYGMALION	with	Julie Andrews
Put to music		Stanley Holloway

<u>MY FAIR LADY</u>

Music by Lerner and Loewe

When Jim came home from the Base that afternoon, I guided him to the table, pointed to the ad and said, "Jim, I really, really want to see this play. May I get tickets for opening night?"

He looked dubious. Sit through two hours of singing and dancing? Do Naval Aviators do that? Probably not. But with the look on my face and the pulsating silence in the room, he shrugged.

"Go ahead." He said something else, but I didn't wait to hear what it was. The tickets were reserved and without realizing it, we saw *FAIR LADY* before it ever opened on Broadway. Even the cast didn't know what they had. Afraid we might miss something, the audience remained standing through most of the performance. When Julie Andrews blew out the candle, the audience cheered and clapped and there were tears on our cheeks. It was a night of absolute magic - even for a Naval Aviator.

The next five years found us moving from Pennsylvania to Georgia, to Florida, to Rhode Island and back to Jacksonville. It was a gypsy life and hard on the children. Flexible as they were, friendships were made and lost on a routine basis, with school continuity lost in the shuffle. We bought houses, sold houses and I learned not to think of them as homes. During that time, our roots were in the fast bags we packed – and each other.

In Geoergia, a beach picnic found Jeff with a large jellyfish wrapped around him and only a quick-thinking Flight Surgeon saved his life by burying him in the sand under salt water. By then, we knew our youngest was accident -prone and we would all age before our time.

In short, we were a family, doing family things. But during the next five years, Jim was more than 'operational' – he was gone. Living on the East Coast, his assignments were to carriers operating in the Mediterranean Sea. The 'cruises' lasted six to seven months and in five years, he would have four Med cruises. I knew women had been saying goodbye to their men for centuries -- that dated back to Biblical times, but this was ridiculous.

So, with Jim's departure, we faced another six months without him. I had to refer to his picture to remember what he looked like.

It wasn't that I sat around and counted the hours he was gone. At one point, he had commented to me, "Busy hands are happy hands" and I almost left him on the spot. Mowing lawns, changing furnace filters, washing windows and doing all the jobs a man does when he's around the house and car, kept my hands not only busy, but looking like a man's hands. I was in danger of losing my sense of gender. I was a woman in a man's world, transients in the civilians' eyes. Here today, gone tomorrow and that made us 'different'. I had learned to resist close friendships. They always ended with a new set of orders and saying so many goodbyes became wearing.

In short, I was lonely.

During his second Med cruise, the parents came to visit and once again. I returned to the theatre I loved. John Van Druten's '*Voice of the Turtle*' ran for three weeks instead of the usual one at the Jacksonville Little Theatre. The time flew by.

For the play, I had gone back to smoking cigarettes, a nasty habit I picked up in college. I quit when I married Jim because he had never smoked and I did not find it hard to give it up. Motivation. But in '*Turtle*', my character did a lot of it. Since 'the play's the thing', I stoked up and after getting over the dizzies, realized it felt good to have a cigarette in my hand. Vowing to quit before Jim came home, I lined up the children and gave them a little talk.

"All right, you two, Daddy's coming home soon and if you don't mind, I would like to tell him myself that I smoked cigarettes for the play.,"

Two heads went up and down. Jeff squirmed, bored with the whole thing, and held firmly onto the cat's tail.

"Jeff, are you paying attention? Did you hear what I asked?

He grinned his famous grin that always made me grin back and said, "I'm not to tell Daddy about your smoking. Right?"

"Right."

The cat finally got loose and took a swipe at him as it fled for the kitchen.

The day the ship came in, we all filed aboard and after the frantic hugs and kisses, crept down the ladder to the Officers' Wardroom below the hangar deck. The long tables were set with white cloths and the smell of coffee from the huge chrome urns, provided a welcome touch. There was 'bug juice', the Navy term for Kool Aid, for the children. We settled at the table to look at each other and begin the game of getting reacquainted. Jeff hooked his arm around his father's, looked up with his enormous gray eyes and grinning his famous grin, said,

"Guess what, Daddy. Mommy smokes."

The silence was profound and I would have liked to pinch his head off. He just needed his father's complete attention, if only for a moment.

He got it.

Patricia Linder

CHAPTER TEN

1959 - 60

We quickly settled into the blissful routine of family life. It had to be quickly because four months later, he left on another six-month - long Med cruise. I never became used to it. My dedication to being a supportive wife, was giving way to being an angry one, left on my own with too many responsibilities. There had never been a divorce in my family and I wasn't about to break the record, but on long, rainy nights with only the cat to keep me warm, I entertained the thought. Usually by morning, it was gone. I worried about the morning it wouldn't be.

Of course he came home from his cruise with a set of orders – War College, Newport, Rhode Island. It would be for less than a year. Two more moves, one up and one back. We were in the double digits by now, and counting. In the meantime, I had accumulated things for the house as women do, and packing became a nightmare, only to be followed by the bigger one of unpacking. But home was important to me. It was our continuity. My husband would come and go often, I would not know where he was, but home sheltered us, took on our personalities and was there when we needed a place to run to. I became quite proficient at making a nest. Our house was livable in less than six hours. The rugs went down, the pictures went up on the wall, the windows were covered, if only temporarily, and coziness set in. I wanted the children to have their things around them as soon as possible. Unpacked crates and boxes are the sign of the transient and we all needed roots.

It was a good year with Jim in War college, studying the art of battle, and all of us together in a little house that was red on the outside and pine paneled on the inside. Even the bathroom had knotholes. At the end of ten months, we packed up and went back to steamy Jacksonville for additional training.

1960

We were still deep into the 'Cold War'. Prior to Jim's Med cruises, the aircraft carrier he was assigned to sailed into Caribbean waters for sea trials or exercises. They weren't just sailing around, enjoying the balmy breezes, they were training for war. Scenarios from the Defense Department provided the ships with the potential problems unique to this kind of conflict. While the American public glanced at their newspapers for information on their investments, the latest in sports and ladies' fashions, the military was preparing for the next move from the Soviet Union. They were very much the enemy, matching us missile for missile, ship for ship, plane for plane. There was no hiatus. The stand-down between World War II and Korea had taught the United States the value of being ready. As strong as Russia was becoming, the threat was serious and real.

The threat at home was one of total frustration. With Thanksgiving a few days away and the ship due back from a month-long exercise off the island of Puerto Rico, none of the wives knew what to do about the turkey.

"Pat, I know it's five o'clock in the morning, but I've got to do something about this turkey before it turns green."

"Pat, have you heard anything? My Jello is melting and the turkey is just sitting there."

"Pat, the kids and I are determined to make this a Thanksgiving he'll never forget. When do I put the turkey in?"

"Pat, I can't keep the children out of the pumpkin pie. Have you had any word on the ship?"

I heard it all.

My civilian friend whose husband supplied the fleet with seafood, called me to say several thousand pounds of shrimp were to be delivered to the pier area by three o'clock that afternoon. The wives were there and waiting when the huge gray ship, slid into its berth. The turkeys came out of the oven right on time and the men never knew how we found out. It was my own version of 'No Need to Know'.

No sooner was the bird demolished, than Jim announced a cross - country to Maine. My safety valve was beginning to rattle. The bloom was definitely off the rose and I felt the familiar tug of anger. Two days later, he arrived back, too late to take the children to the school carnival as promised, and I felt this was a moment of truth. I was geared for battle.

Grinning sheepishly, he said, "Honey, I have a wonderful surprise for you in the garage. But first, we're going to sit down and toast that surprise with a martini."

I cooled down a notch and wondered if my 'wonderful surprise' was a new car. Lord knows, we needed one. The martini was cold and having missed dinner due to the school carnival, it went straight to my head. With pomp and circumstance, we marched through the kitchen, he flung open the door into the garage and flicked on the lights.

Forty-seven live lobsters were crawling around on the floor with only one claw pegged. Being an Iowan, I had never seen a live lobster before.

Words failed me.

"Honey, aren't they beautiful?"

"- - - - - - -."

"Remember how much you like lobster with melted butter?"

"No."

"All we have to do is cook, clean and freeze them. Tomight. Before we go to bed."

"No."

We cooked, cleaned and froze the forty-seven live lobsters he had brought back, stashed in his plane by three o'clock in the morning. At seven AM, the doorbell rang.

A willowy blonde named Heidi smiled into my bleary eyes.

"Hi Pat. Murph said I could stop by for our lobsters this morning. I'm planning a candlelight dinner tonight – melted butter and everything." She smiled coyly and I knew what the 'everything' was.

Lucky Murph. I didn't plan to *speak* to my husband for at least five years.

The pickup procession for lobsters continued throughout the day and the six remaining in the freezer stayed there for months. I was too burned up to cook them.

.When Jim made ready to leave on his third cruise, it became apparent that unless I made some heavy-duty decisions, our marriage was on shaky ground. God and Country took a back seat to proximity. I realized I was married to a man who set records for being away. Something had to change, including my flattened ego.

Jacksonville, 1961

I found a job teaching grade school and made arrangements with our parents to take the children for a month in the summer. Then I announced to Jim, several thousand miles away, that I would be joining him in Italy in June, after school was out and I had the money saved for the trip.

There was no glad shout of joy. He firmly believed in wives staying home and awaiting the warrior's return. An early Commanding Officer had taught him that and he never got over it. But I had had enough of the solitary life. I was no Penelope, weaving her tapestry while waiting for Odysseus to get it all out of his system and come home.

Every Navy wife, if she's smart, will always have a Plan B. It is not mandatory that her husband knows about this – they think their plans are the best anyway – but a woman can't live this kind of life without an alternative. It helps her get around the problems she's stuck with.

My Plan B went into overdrive the moment it was made. Finding a job was no problem. The citizens of Dade County, Florida had not seen fit to vote the school bond issue and the teachers left the area like lemmings for the sea. The schools were crumbling, segregation was rampant and as the Superintendent said when I applied,

"If you can spell your own name and know the alphabet, you know more than your students do." He was talking about seventh and eighth graders.

It was not an easy year, but I was motivated. Every pay- check went into a savings account and the reward at the end was Italy and my husband. The experience taught me more about myself than anything the students learned from me. Although, in my home- room class, out of the six boys on probation from reform school, (they always assigned them to the newest teacher), three decided at the end of the year to go on to High School. I counted that as a personal triumph, despite the daily frisking for weapons which had to be handed back at the end of their last class.

Talents were discovered. Mine. I could break up a race riot in seven minutes flat. My school was on the street the black students took to get to their school. Every morning, there was a racial confrontation. Every morning I waded in, arbitrated and broke it up. This automatically exempted me from Hall Monitor and cafeteria duty and I would have done anything to get out of that. I even learned I could make friends with a baby alligator, recovered from the swamp by one of my 'slower' students who lived with her grandparents. She fit the Superintendent's category of not knowing the alphabet, and how she made it to the eighth grade was a mystery, but she thought I was her Mama and brought me the alligator as a gesture of love. It scuttled around next to my desk until it outgrew its chicken wire cage, then returned to the swamp, by way of her burly grandfather.

It all worked out somehow. The year ended, the children left for Iowa and the grandparents, I withdrew my savings and bought my ticket to Naples, Italy.

The carrier anchored five miles off Naples and I went to the airport to meet Jim when he flew in from the ship.

He walked right past me.

The year of teaching had thinned me down and after all, it had been quite a while since we had seen each other. If I had any doubts about what I was doing there instead of staying at home, I lost them in that instant. We had a lot of mending to do and it would begin with getting reacquainted.

We had our moments. In the little town of Brig, on the way to Zermatt, Switzerland, Jim left the train to check on our tickets. Since he had our money, passports and rail tickets, when the train began to move with him nowhere in sight, I threw all the luggage out the window and to the delight of the watching passengers, jumped off the train. It was the only time I ever heard him swear blue.

I was out of my element. This little Iowa girl had never been outside the United States and although the past ten years had shaped, formed and toughened me, they hadn't prepared me for life alone in a foreign country. When the carrier put into port, Jim took as much leave as he was allowed and we traveled through Italy.

He was always uneasy.

Ships had been known to leave suddenly, due to operational demands and this was in the back of his mind. But I was there, had worked hard, saved my money and deserved some of his time. Too soon, the ship demanded and he left me in Florence, Italy in a little pensione called The Argentina.

"Jim, I'm a little anxious about being here alone. If I knew the language, there wouldn't be a problem, but I really don't know how I'm going to handle this."

"You'll be fine, kiddo. You can do anything you want to, within reason. Just ask the concierge for directions and try to remember how to get back."

I just didn't want him to go. "That concierge is related to the Borgias and I'll bet she'll make me stay in every night and eat tough veal by myself in the courtyard."

"I've tipped her pretty well and explained the situation. You can spend the next five days in the Ufizzi Gallery without any complaints from me."

I think I'll just go look at Michelangelo's David, instead."

Jim grinned. "Gotta go. Love you." Gone.

The days were glorious. I walked Florence, paid the Uffizi Gallery a visit every day until the guards began to follow me, strolled the Ponte Vecchio bridge and sought out every Michelangelo I could find. It was my first visit, but not my last. Communication was through smiles, hand gestures and a lot of shoulder shrugging. There was no problem. The universal language kicked in and because of my very limited funds, shopping was kept at a minimum. True to her Borgia background, the Concierge insisted I stay in every night and eat tough veal alone in the courtyard. Whatever. I knew with certainty, I would return to this place.

'See Naples and die' and it was up to me to find my way back to it. All I could afford was second class on the train to Livorno, then another train to Rome, then Naples. Leaving the station, I hung out the window with everybody else, saying 'Caio' to the crowd on the platform. Why not, they were saying it to me. I loved this country.

"Pepeeeeeeeno." She was a heavy-set woman who came out of the cave three times a day, to sit on a three-legged stool. With a great bowl of spaghetti in her lap (no sauce), one fork and a voice that could reach to Vesuvius across the bay, she called her brood — Peppino being the one that never turned up. I watched as the children flocked to her, opened their mouths like swallows on the wing, for a forkful of spaghetti, then raced away until hunger gnawed again. The caves lined the streets in parts of Naples and had been used as homes for centuries.

She gave it another try, "Peppeeeeeeeeno" .

I missed the children

A lot.

CHAPTER ELEVEN

1961 - 62

There was one more cruise to go, but after my sojourn in Europe, and the renewal it brought to both of us, it would be a piece of cake. I felt strong and sure of myself. Bumming around the Continent was not, in those pre-sixties days, something one did blithely. With no language skills and no sense of direction, I got there and back, passed GO and did not end up in jail. My mother had warned me about 'white slavers', but the Neapolitans convinced me that life is just a lineful of laundry over a narrow cobbled street full of highly emotional people who would rather pinch you than kidnap you.

Back in Jacksonville, accumulated mail produced a letter from the Board of Education, offering me a job as head of the English Department for a brand new school opening in the fall. When I saw the return address on the envelope, I wondered if they were coming after me for teaching without any Education credits or degrees. Maybe they were impressed with my riot tactics or my affinity for alligators. Whatever it was, I responded I would like to take a look at the school and my classroom, in particular. My last one had the electrical wiring hanging out of the walls where my six 'bad boys' dug away the plaster and periodically, shorted out the entire school. That was *before* I confiscated their weapons.

With Jamey and Jeff, I toured the school, resplendent with the smell of new plaster, tile adhesive and soft, pastel paint. It was a teacher's dream —come- true. In my absence, the school bond issue was voted through and the city was making up for past transgressions. I would even have a 'lab' for the slower students. It was one heady experience and with my newly discovered self-assurance, I knew I could lick my weight in eighth and ninth-graders. Hands down.

A tug on my skirt and a small voice said, "Mom, do you *have* to teach?"

Jeff looked up at me with eyes like his father's. His scars were nearly gone, except to me. He was eight years old and the year before, he came home from school ten minutes before I did.

"Why, Jeff?'

"Because I don't want to be a latch-key-kid anymore. I want to come home and have you be there."

Without further thought, I said, "I'll be there, Jeff." This little guy could talk me out of anything.

It was a wrench and I sometimes wondered what I had missed, passing up the opportunity. But we do what we have to do and it was the right decision. I was solely responsible for these two little lives and what they became, depended on my decisions – right or wrong. There was another person in our family who also depended on my judgement, and the words he had learned at the Navy's knee, "There's no such thing as an excuse," left no doubt in my mind as to my actions.

Not to dwell on regrets, I volunteered. The Red Cross was always looking for warm bodies to help in the Naval Hospital and after taking the indoctrination course which left me totally unmotivated, I signed on anyway and was sent to the Orthopedic Post- Surgical Ward.

I called them my 'Bone Boys'. They were, for the most part, young sailors, fresh off their smashed motorcycles and learning to live without arms or legs. An angry doctor had hung framed photographs of destroyed motorcycles on the walls. He was weary of cutting off appendages on young men and that was his statement. They were an unruly bunch. Their macho was gone. Only their shaken egos remained to sustain them as men. That, and a false bravado. They were frightened.

When I first appeared in my starched, gray striped uniform with white cap and the insignia that represents compassion the world over, they, as one, gave this 'pigeon' a hard time. But this pigeon turned out to be a tough old bird and by my second visit, we had established rapport. When they ruffled my feathers, I ruffled theirs. They loved it. I treated them as normal, with everything intact and the day the hospital gave its permission for a wheelchair race down the long concrete walkway, I was theirs. They knew I would fight for them to get whatever they needed desperately. The hospital provided the medicines for their bodies and I worked on their psyches.

But the day I introduced them to Shakespeare, perched on a high stool, I was met by catcalls and whistles. No matter. I reminded them they were a captive audience and got a pillow past my left ear.

Hamlet grabbed them, Macbeth spun them and Lear left them limp. They were hooked and I was having another wonderful day on the stage.

One fragile boy would go back to his home in the West Virginia mountains with no legs at all. He was always quiet, didn't enter in and his eyes looked inward as though he had quit on life. I wondered about his future in those poor hills. He liked poetry and I read Emily Dickinson to him – a poem a day. It was the only thing that reached him

> The clouds their backs together laid,
>
> The north began to push,
>
> The forests galloped till they fell,
>
> The lightning skipped like mice;
>
> The thunder crumbled like a stuff ---
>
> How good to be safe in tombs,
>
> Where nature's temper cannot reach,
>
> Nor vengeance ever comes!
>
> *Emily Dickinson LX*

I pondered the boy's choice and wondered if that was what he really dreamed of – to be gone from life. But aside from compassion and friendship, I could offer him nothing that would penetrate the pain I saw in his eyes. It became increasingly difficult to let go of these Bone Boys as they hobbled off to God knows what. I never noticed the time as it sped by.

I was asked to substitute in Outpatient Surgery on a hot Wednesday afternoon and our third customer was a man with a mean-looking carbuncle on his neck. He hurt – a lot, and as I sprayed anaesthetic on the offending area, a group of squadron wives entered the post-op room to 'observe'. They had been cleared for a visit and fresh from a luncheon in hats and gloves, they gathered a respectful distance away. Funds were being raised for some badly needed pieces of hospital equipment and they were involved in the mechanics of the fund-raiser. The Commanding Officer's wife was wearing a large round cartwheel hat. The doctor stepped up to the now numbed neck and with a scalpel, penetrated the carbuncle. As the trapped green fluid shot skyward, the CO's wife slowly sank to the floor in a dead faint and the hat went rolling down the corridor. Struck dumb is a good description of all involved and only after the ministrations of a disgusted Navy nurse, was the lady able to depart the room and find her hat.

The Red Cross was to serve me well in the years to come. I would need them and they would need me.

Throughout these times of travel, cruises and raising children, the world continued to turn. 1961 – 62 were years to remember and the nation thrilled and chilled to the events as they formed and passed into history. In 1961, the Soviet Union sealed off East Germany with the Berlin Wall and divided seemingly forever, a country still struggling to recover from the war it had so methodically begun. John F. Kennedy was elected President, only to be met by the ill-fated Bay of Pigs on Cuba's shore. Fidel Castro displayed his thug-like charm and propensity to Communism and drove the State Department crazy. Space exploration kicked into high gear with the Soviet Union getting the drop on us when Cosmonout Yuri Gagarin became the first human to enter space. The heavens were getting littered with satellites, big and small, theirs and ours. It was exciting.

The week before Jim returned from his final cruise of the set of four, my neighbor nervously called me to ask if I had any extra blankets she could soak with water and hang on her back fence to keep the wildfire from her back yard. The tinder-dry meadow behind her house was burning at a furious rate and headed straight for our street. Sidestepping the snakes that were racing ahead of the fire, we soaked and hung the blankets on the chain-link fence and with brooms, beat out the flames as they jumped the fence. The snakes were a bigger problem, holing up in garages and front porches. But the next day, with the fire out, we watched an army of chinch bugs destroy one lawn after another, including ours as they marched down the block.

Of course, Jim missed all this. If there was an emergency, be it broken washing machines, dented fenders or hungry chinch bugs, he was at sea. It was a Navy wife's lot and the gods always waited until the ship sailed to throw their thunderbolts. After all, Mars, the god of war was a male and they do stick together.

It was time for the end of another long cruise and another homecoming. I had been through so many, I wondered if I could summon up any of the magic of the first one, so many years ago.

No matter what the men have been doing during those months away, nosing into a familiar pier with women and children dressed in their Sunday best, eyes searching every face for that one familiar one, can only be uniquely exciting to a man. For the married ones, family life will begin again. Exotic gifts will spill onto the floor of a shiny house, made ready for his homecoming by wife and children alike. Eyes meet and look away – embarrassed by the prospect of intimacy with a stranger. Children vie for his attention, then with the fact established that he is *home*, they scatter to their childish pursuits and the comfort of a man's castle is his to savor.

Not every homecoming is idyllic. In the floating city of 5,000 Navy men, parents die, divorces are filed or become final and 'Dear John' letters are received and dealt with. But for the men with no one waiting for them on the dock, the loneliness of the sea pales against the emptiness of no one to touch. However, the cocky sailor will forever be cocky. The tilt of his hat proves it. They disembark with swagger and purpose, bellbottoms skin tight, and you know they won't be alone for long.

For a man and his wife, the feeling is complex. People change in seven months. Wives grow new lines around the eyes, the children sprout and begin to bud out. Young girls turn into women and to their fathers, the prospect is not only startling, but unsettling. There will be more cruises and children at any age need a man's protection and interest. But for the moment, the business of family living becomes exciting and fulfilling. Each couple celebrates it in their own way, with only the newness of the shared experience as their common denominator.

The temptation to tell about the chinch bugs, fires, snakes and the broken washing machine, waits until he can absorb the good stuff. Best not to bring up the note from the teacher. Give the kids a chance to make their position with Dad a solid one. The rules are endless and after enough of these cruises, you realize you are on your best behavior and so is he. Even the children haul out manners you didn't know they had. You are different people than you were yesterday and the word 'façade' comes to mind.

`They zipped up John Glenn into his flight suit and poured him into the Mercury Space Capsule that would fling him into space and take him once around the world. Jim was chosen to lead a flight to return all information and data associated with the recovery to Patrick Air Force Base. The children and I watched from the back yard as the Mercury shot skyward from Cape Canaveral and I knew Jim relished having even a small part in such an important scientific event.

CHAPTER TWELVE

1962

"Pat. Walter called from the Intelligence Center and said we could be under attack in a matter of hours."

I was so shocked, I couldn't think of anything to say.

We were snug in a three-bedroom rental in Washington, D.C. Jim had been operational for so long, he was now paying the price – a desk job that he considered 'the pound of flesh.'

John F. Kennedy was our President and between the Bay of Pigs and the Cuban Missile Crisis, it was a tense time for the United States. Our neighbor Walter, worked at Arlington Hall (Army Intelligence Center), generally known as Spook Country. The day before the Cuban missile stand down, his wife Bonnie, called to say she had heard from her husband.

After delivering the news of an impending attack, she continued breathlessly, "He also told me to put all our canned food and bottles of water downstairs. Bring our sheets and pillowcases down there, too. We might need them for bandages."

Bandages! My God, this would be a nuclear attack and according to Walter, we would soon be nothing but a mess of loose molecules. But it gave me something to do, After dutifully putting the canned goods and bottles of water in the lower level of our split-level house, I set up the ironing board and ironed all our sheets. My mother always said, "Patti, ironed sheets and clean underwear, in case of an emergency." I never questioned the logic, I just made sure we had both.

The problem with ironing is that it provides time to think. As the wrinkles disappeared on the sheets, they increased in my thoughts. I had lived long enough with the military to know the potential might of our arch -enemy, Russia. I had an idea of what 'nuclear attack' meant. Put together, they spelled the end of life as we knew it. More simply -- the end. And we were living at ground zero. I forced myself to keep thoughts of our children out of my mind. By some miracle, they would go on to live their lives. I was sure of it. The whole thing was like being told by the doctor that you have two or three days left to live. Where do you start? I had absolutely no answers, other than the faith that had gotten us this far, would take us on through whatever happened next. Over in a flash – no pain, no conscious thought – just over. Unconnected thoughts moved around in my head; Thy will be done…..here today, gone tomorrow…….this too, shall pass……..always leave 'em laughing. And the iron glided on.

A large group of mothers met the school bus and we hurried our children home, numb to the thought of our puny efforts to stave off total annihilation. We waited for the other shoe to drop. There was no telephone communication between Jim and me – a habit spawned by the Med cruises – one I never questioned, but one I didn't like. Military lines had to be kept open and free of unnecessary calls. Rules were rules and if we all ended up vaporized, a phone call would hardly help, anyway.

On October 22 1962, President Kennedy announced the naval blockade of Cuba, as a result of the Soviet Union shipments of nuclear weapons to that country. For months, air intelligence had spotted ballistic missile installations and the uncrating and assembling of Soviet -made jet bombers. The nuclear missiles were of the 1,000 to 2,000 mile range, putting the entire East Coast in jeopardy. Washington, D.C. was the prime target. It was a perfect example of Cold War tactics. Nikita Krushchev, Premier of the Soviet Union had surreptitiously sneaked in the weapons necessary to wipe out the eastern part of the United States.

He assumed we would do nothing about it.

The military went on full alert, as Kennedy ordered the Armed Forces to "prepare for any eventuality." Forty ships and 20,000 men moved into position for the blockade. The President received full support from Congress and presented Krushchev with an ultimatum that in effect said: *Take your missiles and your planes and get the hell out of Cuba or you will be facing all out war. Period.*

For four tense days, we waited for the big bang. Jim was assigned to the Bureau of Personnel (BUPERS). It is people who do the job and any quick mobilization requires a thorough knowledge of who is qualified and available at a moment's notice. As a military wife, you know the possibilities of your husband going into harm's way, but you also know it's his job.

As I hauled the stashed canned goods up the stairs for dinner with the children, I could imagine Jim's frustration at being nailed to a desk, instead of sitting in a plane on the flight deck of a carrier in the

Caribbean Sea, awaiting launch orders over Cuba. That was the real 'pound of flesh'.

As we all know, it ended with the withdrawal of the missiles and planes, a chastened and wiser Krushchev who could do little more than pound his shoe on the desk at the United Nations and an angry Castro who was furious that his Communist buddy had caved in so easily. For the American public, complacent with the peacetime of the early Sixties, it was a demonstration of the military's ability to respond immediately to a national crisis. For our family, it was business as usual as Jim finally came home for eight hours of untroubled sleep.

I approached the Red Cross, donned my pin-stripe uniform and began my teaching of the handicapped at the George Mason School for Exceptional Children. These were children born with Down Syndrome, autism or severe epilepsy. Once I learned the words to *'Puff, the Magic Dragon'*, their favorite song, it became an exhausting but rewarding way to spend my days.

Midway in his tour of duty at BUPERS, Jim was selected to become an Admiral's Aide.

Now there's a world!

Resplendent in the gold braid (often referred to as 'idiot loops') that announces their job, Navy Aides assume the position of two steps behind and one to the side.

I particularly enjoyed that, having been there for most of my married life.

They are in attendance at all times the Admiral is awake and moving, and at parties with more than one Admiral, the Aides circle their wagons and assume The Position –arms akimbo, or extended with hands crossed over each other, ending in a fairly strategic area of their anatomy. We were lucky. Admiral William Smedberg was a lovely man with an equally warm and friendly wife and we felt more like their children than just a junior rank couple.

The job placed us in the heady atmosphere of the 'upper echelon' with conversations centered on the Washington scene, the Navy and the big picture of the military structure of our country. Every branch of the service has its unique problems. The world was changing and as it does, so do the particular needs of its defense. I knew   the cardinal rule for a Navy wife – 'Don't make waves' -- so, at parties and dinners, I listened to the male conversations and tried to learn as much as I could about this tight little island we inhabited. Cautious words of war made me realize that new orders for Jim would come through within the year, but not wanting to assume the worst, I focused on the bigger picture.

Capitol Hill, for some unexplained reason, felt like home ground to me. I walked the halls, marveled at the acoustics in the Capitol rotunda, made my way to the Senate and settled in to watch our monolithic government at work.

Everett McKinley Dirksen, growling out hellos, strode into the Senate chambers and down the aisle toward his seat. Democrats and Republicans alike rose and moved to greet him. His gravelly voice carried humor, wit and intelligence. The Republican Minority Whip was revered by all and for this Republicans from Iowa, I was delighted to watch the bear of a man from our neighboring state of Illinois.

Once in session, several Senators rose to complain about the deepening snow and ask that they be let out early to go home. True, the Christmas holidays were approaching, but there was important legislation on the floor to be considered and they sounded like unruly school boys. Everett Dirksen just sat quietly and shook his shaggy head.

On the day President Kennedy was assassinated, Jim was with Admiral Smedberg, attending a conference at the War College in Newport, Rhode Island. As the Superintendent of the College spoke to the attending Admirals, his secretary interrupted his speech with the news of the President's death. Shaken, he made the stunning announcement and immediately, the gathered Aides moved forward, ready to escort their Admirals to the plane.

Jim asked, "Admiral Smedberg, do you wish to leave for Washington now?"

"Sit down, Commander. We will remain here until we have heard the rest of Admiral Austin's address."

Logically, it made sense, but emotionally, it was a very hard task, indeed. The Commander-in-Chief was dead and in Navy terms, the ship was without a rudder. The Admirals returned to Washington later in the day, but events were moving swiftly and with Vice President Johnson ready to step into the Presidency, there were no calls for 'Battle Stations'. Security was tightened and there was an air of vigilance, borne of shock. The immense Washington bureaucracy paused in its sluggish snail-like pace, then despite the frenzied hysteria of the media, returned to 'business as usual'.

Surprisingly, Jim came home that night. They had flown back to Washington and   returned to Admiral Smedberg's office. Calls were put in to the Secretary of the Navy (SECNAV), the Chief of Naval Operations (CNO) and many others, requesting that calm be maintained.

Jim told me later, "Sometimes, the other aides and I would stand in my office at the big window overlooking Arlington Cemetery and joke about that being the alternative to a bad day. But today, I looked at the rows of white crosses and knew the President would soon be joining the men who chose to remain there. It was a sobering thought."

"What about Admiral Smedberg? Did he say anything about that?"

He smiled. "No. 'Smeddy' just told us to go home to our families."

For me, work at the school had been demanding that November day and I was tired. Hurrying to be home when the school bus dropped off our children, I heard the announcement on the car radio. I took the first exit off the freeway; found a place I could stop and stared at my hands as they held onto the steering wheel. Politics didn't matter. The President was dead and I felt bereft – robbed. In this world of FBI and CIA, where was everybody? The words,

'Secret Service' kept echoing in my head and inanely I thought, 'Is this what our tax dollars pay for? No protection for the President?' Immediately, I was ashamed for having such an erroneous thought. It was a knee-jerk reaction of anger. I had watched those Secret Service men at work on many occasions and felt only admiration for their willingness to put themselves between death and the man they guarded.

I knew I must be home before the children arrived home from school. Once again, there was a large group of mothers at the bus stop. But this time, when the doors opened and the children emerged, every child was weeping. We gathered them up and fled for the sanity that home offered. When Jim finally came home that night, we talked together with the children and tried to explain how such a thing could happen. Washington was providing them with a pretty shabby view of our country. I could feel my own illusions wavering and only hoped their youth would let them forget the horror and remember only the man.

CHAPTER THIRTEEN

1964

The expected new orders read,'VA-43, NAS Oceana, Virginia RP/RAG Training. The date was August 1964, the same month the Vietnam War began for the U.S. in the Tonkin Gulf.

VA-43 was an Air Group replacement training squadron for pilots who had held down desk jobs for the past year or so. Its designation was 'Light Attack' and the planes were A-4 's -- single pilot jets otherwise called the Skyhawk. The men fondly referred to them as 'Scooters' ; the wives tried not to refer to them at all. They looked like mosquitoes when parked on the runway. There was no RIO (radar intercept officer) in the back seat, because there was no back seat. The pilot who climbs into its cockpit has only God and a bevy of instruments as company. Over a rice paddy, with a SAM missile on your tail, you hope neither one will fail you.

I knew something was up when the sparkle returned to Jim's eyes. Being part of the Bureau of Personnel, he probably knew before anyone else that he was about to become 'Operational' once again. In this case, Operational meant combat.

Sure, there was a war out there someplace in the far reaches of Southeast Asia, but it had been going on since 1959 and it was a war between the French and their colony, Vietnam. Not to worry. It's their war, not ours. Right?

Wrong.

The French finally pulled out after years of fighting in the dense, steaming jungles of the small country, leaving South Vietnam anti-communist and North Vietnam a communist appendage of China and Russia. It was a war, waiting to happen. Supplied by the two red giants to the north, North Vietnam made ready to absorb its southern counterpart.

But the United States, always on the alert when an anti-Communist government resists being taken over by the bad guys, sent advisers, military assistance and diplomatic support to the little country south of the 17th parallel to hold out as long as they could. Before his death, President Kennedy had watched the scenario unfold and despite President Eisenhower's advice to 'stay out of a war in Asia', it soon became obvious to President Johnson, Kennedy's successor, that unless we intervened, all of Southeast Asia would fall into the communist giants' hands.

In 1965, we went to war in a country thousands of miles away.. The domino theory was introduced -- once one country falls to communism, they all will. But the spreading cancer of communism was passe` – gone with the McCarthy era. The American public with the help of the media, rejected the whole concept.

Naval Air Station Oceana is a master jet base, just down the road from Virginia Beach. The children and I drove down to house-hunt and found very little of any worth. Developers were throwing up matchboxes that would hardly withstand a good blow, let alone a hurricane. The prices were through the ceiling. Jim flew down, found a beautiful home, bought it and we moved into what the children called "The White House", a home we would keep for thirty years. We loved the hardwood floors, curving driveway, dogwoods and tall pines that routinely shed piles of needles. Of course the mortgage reached into infinity, but this was the second really pretty house we had ever owned and a joy to put together.

Jim reported as an RP (replacement pilot) to Squadron 43 for Replacement Air Group training. Anyone with a grain of sense knew what that meant. Aircraft carriers would be going to Vietnam with Air Groups aboard. Air Groups are made up of squadrons of planes – all kinds – and it takes men to fly them. Although the war did not officially begin until 1965, the provocation of the Gulf of Tonkin incident made it crystal clear we would participate on more than an observatory level. President Johnson committed the United States to the use of ground troops and intensive bombing, and the military made ready to go to war. All of this without the sanction of Congress.

Two weeks later, Jim called from the base to say there was a note on the bulletin board that the squadron he was attached to would move to Florida.. For the first time in my fifteen years as a Navy wife, I said, "No."

The children were in good schools with a possibility of remaining long enough to make friends and in time, they would get over leaving the ones behind in Washington. I had the house of my dreams and I was tired of being shoved from one place to another with no seeming regard for the other three lives that made up our family. Others we knew had remained behind to retain the continuity of the children's schooling, but until now, I had resisted that. The family as a unit had always been our strength. But I wasn't dealing with little children anymore. Their worlds were as important to them as their father's was to him. Trying to understand the abstract of a Naval career and its demands, held little weight to a fourteen-year-old, having to prove herself in her first year of high school. There was enough maturity in our children because of their way of life, they deserved consideration.

We talked about these things and waited for the change of orders to come. They never did. The notice remained on the bulletin board, but the squadron remained at Oceana. It was somewhat akin to Chinese water torture – the drip, drip, drip of possibility.

The training lasted four months, then Jim was given orders to Attack Squadron VA76, scheduled to go to the Mediterranean area when it returned from its Vietnam tour. .Jim first joined the squadron as its Executive Officer, then 'fleeted' up to Commanding Officer. When I learned the Change of Command would be held in Lemoore, California, due to Vietnam rotation, I decided to surprise my husband by being there when he took command of the squadron. He had been on the West Coast, operating with '76 and I saw the chance for us to be together, even for a few days.

A good friend offered to have our children join her family for the time I would be gone and I carefully packed my best clothes for the ceremony. It was a long flight from Norfolk to San Francisco, then a connecting flight to Fresno, north of Lemoore. I had to tell Jim I was coming. Driving was the only way to get to the Naval Base. At midnight, my flight arrived in Fresno.

No Jim.

Not only no Jim, but my luggage was in San Francisco with the possibility of going on to Honolulu within a few hours. It was shaping up to be the nightmare journey of the year. After an hour, Jim sheepishly arrived, explaining the squadron had given a party for the outgoing and incoming commanding officers. He had no idea how long it would take to make the drive from Lemoore to Fresno, but assumed thirty minutes should do it. Never assume a damned thing – never. His own words.

'Steamed' is a good description of my attitude at that moment. I told him of my lost luggage, my loss of good humor and my determination to get on the next flight home. He smoothed my ruffled feathers, made sure my luggage would be there for pickup at six o'clock in the morning, then steered me out the door to the nearest motel.

The Change of Command was at nine o'clock and we would still have to drive back to Lemoore.

The motel was grim, suiting my mood. Jim looked around, took two quarters out of his pocket and deposited them in the vibrating bed.

Clutching my purse, the only piece of luggage I still had left, I said, "What on earth are you doing?"

He actually looked like a spanked puppy. "I thought the vibrator might relax you after the long trip."

"Jim, I have been vibrating on an airplane for nine hours. I do not want to get into that bed." Not only was it going sideways, it was going up and down.

"I don't know how to turn it off."

"The plug, dear. Pull the plug."

"That might break it and I don't have enough money on me to pay for a broken vibrating bed."

"PULL.   THE.   PLUG."

The plug was pulled. I considered making up *his* bed in the bathtub, but needed a shower more. Six AM, with luggage in hand, we sped back to Lemoore as I changed into my other clothes in the car.

At precisely nine o'clock, dressed appropriately – Jim in his uniform, shoes shined and I in my finery, we sedately walked into the hangar. Jim went to the platform and I to my seat in the front row. Not a hair out of place.

Much to my astonishment, upon accepting the command of the squadron, Jim spoke feelingly about having a wife who would travel so many miles to attend this important day in his life. He did not mention the vibrating bed.

He brought his squadron back to Virginia Beach, having been given orders to report to the carrier, America, stationed on the East Coast, for a tour to the Mediterranean Sea.

At a cocktail party one evening, a few weeks later, the Commanding Officer of the carrier, Enterprise, a West Coast based ship, casually mentioned that Jim's squadron had just been assigned to his ship and would be leaving for Vietnam, instead of the Mediterraean.   In a matter of seconds, my husband went from relative safety to deadly combat. I went home with a headache.

Squadron VA 76 moved back to the West Coast and made ready for war. The wives remained in Virginia Beach and settled in to wait it out.

Ji,m's squadron was attached to an air Group based in California, and that left us a continent away from any kind of support. Lack of communication was the hardest to bear. We knew if our men were shot down, someone would find us to deliver the news, but for family emergencies, we were on our own. We were a tightly-knit group of women – meeting often and sharing what came through in letters from our husbands.

The Navy's term for North Vietnam, was Yankee Station.. When the carriers launched strikes over the enemy, they were on Yankee Station. They rotated – so many weeks in the north, then south to Dixie Station, while another carrier moved into strike position.

It was nearing Christmas. The children and I opted for Sunday dinner at a nearby restaurant – old, traditional with the grace of the deep South in its décor and food.

The phone rang minutes before we were to leave with the message that one of the pilots of VA 76 had been shot down over enemy territory. The pilot's body had been sighted on a hillside by his wingman and passes were being made to determine if he could be rescued. His wife would be told and I would be kept informed.

I chose to keep this piece of information to myself. All my acting training in the theatre kicked in that afternoon as we consulted the menu, debated over shrimp versus fried chicken, remarked on the Christmas decorations and in general, had a special kind of time with each other. My protective instincts were in high gear. These children were to be spared. There would be many times like this ahead of us. I knew it was up to me to keep Jamey and Jeff's lives steady.

Later that day, I met with the young pilot's wife. Her luminous blue eyes were shadowed with sadness and fear. Her hands, palms up, lay limp in her lap. We could do nothing but wait for the next set of information. When it came, it was not good.

"Millie, they're sure now that Mac's not alive."

"Will they just leave him there?" She closed her eyes and when once again, they opened, they were so full of pain, I had to look away.

I knew she wanted the truth. "That's a possibility. The Viet Cong have booby-trapped his body. There is a lot of enemy fire in that area and they were only able to send in a helicopter to identify him as one of ours. Our men can't conduct rescue efforts because of the intensity of the anti-aircraft that's all around him. Essentially, the Viet Cong is using Mac as bait." The Navy would eventually tell her this, but coming from another woman, although the words were blunt, they were honest. I knew she trusted me to level with her.

She walked to the window and stood quietly for a few moments. Then I heard her say in a voice that was only a whisper, "But it's raining on him. He'll be so cold and wet."

War is hell.

In a few days' time, Millie opted to return to her parents, and in a last effort to leave her with some kind of peace, I visited the Base Chaplain with the request that a Catholic mass be said for the lost young pilot. The phone on the Chaplain's desk rang softly and excusing himself, he turned from me to answer it. After a moment of silence as he listened, he glanced at me, then swung his chair around to face the wall. I waited in the quiet room. Slowly, he pivoted back to face his desk. Avoiding my eyes, he spoke carefully, "Mrs. Linder, they have just reported that your husband, Commander Linder has been shot down over Hanoi."

I stared at him for what seemed like a very long time, then said, "No Chaplain, he has not."

A swift denial, but the image of my children's faces as I delivered the news, prompted me to say, "Please call back and confirm."

He did so immediately and indeed, the information was incorrect. Another squadron CO was down with a squadron number that sounded like '76. He had been a good friend.

Millie's plane was scheduled to leave within an hour. Once in the car, I hurried to the airport, only to be stopped by a patrolman, given a lecture on driving forty miles an hour in a thirty-five mile an hour zone and told to report to the courthouse two weeks later. I missed the plane and Millie took off alone without even a proper goodbye.

The children looked different to me that night. I studied them as they studied their homework. The erroneous message had brought me up short. There, but for the grace of God, go I. It might come but was I prepared? As my protective shell was turning into concrete, I wondered if human feelings would ever escape. The children looked to me to give them something more than death and destruction in their young lives. One step at a time – one day at a time – no looking ahead because what's out there is not nice.

CHAPTER FOURTEEN

Two weeks later, I had my day in court. Because I was on duty at the Oceana Dispensary, I wore my Red Cross uniform with the intention of going directly from Court to the Air Station and an afternoon's work with sick dependents.

In the courtroom, after listening to sobered -up drunk drivers whine away the morning, my turn finally came. I approached the bench and told my story. When I finished, the Clerk of the Court was weeping into her handkerchief, the recorder was trying to see through her tears to get it all down and the Judge, bless him, blew his nose, then wiped his eyes. However, I was gently – very gently admonished about speeding. My fine was $25.00. I didn't mind. The law had been broken and I gladly paid my dues.

What mattered most was the Judge ending his softly spoken lecture with the words, "Mrs. Linder, we are all so sorry and I speak for the whole court. We hope this never happens to you."

I felt good when I left. There was a room full of civilians who were a little wiser in the ways of war, especially when it's on their own doorstep.

It proved to be quite a day. Instead of the Dispensary, I found a Red Cross Field Director waiting for me and after driving to the man's office on the Base, I was asked to become the Chairman of Volunteers for the Oceana Naval Base. Being wartime, it was a big job, but I didn't hesitate. I would be busy – too busy to dwell on the

115

war news of the day. After a thorough briefing on my duties, the Director left. I wondered what next.

What next was a woman with her three children, all under the age of six, who sidled shyly into the room, parked her children on three chairs and approached the desk. Hesitantly, she softly asked, "Ma'am? Does the Red Cross have a swimming pool for handicapped children?"

My gaze went from a care-worn, tired face with haunted eyes, to the three faces across the room. The two younger ones were staring intently at me. The six-year-old was staring at nothing. She was blind.

"Mrs.....?"

"Yaeger."

"Mrs. Yaeger, sit here next to my desk and we'll find out right now."

She sank into the chair and sat with hands folded in her lap. Calling the main Red Cross office in downtown Norfolk, I asked my question then regretfully told Mrs. Yaeger, "No, I'm afraid not." She was obviously a Navy dependent or she wouldn't be here in my office. We began to talk.

"Mrs. Yaeger, are you asking for yourself or for a friend?" I knew the one child was blind, but I sensed there was more to be told.

"No, for myself. My oldest, Marie, is six and she went blind about three months ago. The doctor says my other two will be blind by the time they're six, too."

I felt like someone had punched me in the stomach.

"My dear, I am so sorry. Is this an inherited problem?"

"That's how the tests came out. My husband's a sailor on a destroyer and when the doctor told us about the other two, he took off with the car and most of our money and he's now UA. We're just about out of everything. But the kids want to swim and I thought I would try to find out if there was a free pool."

I wished I had my hands around 'unauthorized absence' Seaman Yaeger's throat

A call to the Navy Relief office on the Bas was next. The NavyRelief Society is a privately funded organization that provides food, clothing, money and services for Navy families in need. They handle emergencies, set up loans and all Seaman Yaeger had to do was dial their number. Instead, he chose to run. I sincerely hoped the Navy caught him and gave him brig time for the next fifty years.

More calls were made and by now, Mrs. Yaeger was Sophie, Marie was on a chair by my desk, Lucy was exploring my top drawer and Ralphie was on my lap. Things began to happen. Within the hour, Sophie and her brood were driven home with a stop at the grocery store and a promise from me to call that night. Shee had an appointment with the Red Cross for the next morning.

What I found in my follow-up calls, staggered me. There was only one school for the blind in all of the Hampton Roads (seven cities) area and it was for black children. White children would have a hard time getting in. There was no special education for blind children.. They rode the same school buses and attended the same classes as seeing children did. Further, there were no special facilities for Navy dependents with handicaps or special needs. Ignoring the other seven cities – they were big enough and rich enough to take care of their own --I decided to concentrate on providing for Navy dependents, beginning with Sophie.

Sophie lived just a few short blocks from us. For the next three weeks, I worked with the Red Cross and Navy Relief. Between us, we found Sophie's family in San Francisco, arranged for her transportation, new clothes all around, and sent her home with information on what medical help was available for her children in California.

Sophie and her children had become a part of our family in those three weeks and I felt truly lost as they excitedly marched onto the plane, Marie holding tightly to her mother's skirt. Things went well for Sophie in San Francisco. She was a strong woman and although all of her children were blind by the age of six, they managed to live normal lives with the help of her family. Hopefully, Seaman Yeager is still languishing in a dark and airless brig.

Because of a retarded sister, President John F. Kennedy brought light to retarded children who had been relegated to the inside of a house or in some cases, closets when there were strangers about. Tradition decreed they be kept out of sight. That changed in the early Sixties and the closet doors were opened. Slowly, the bleak and hopeless picture began to change. Dedicated people, often using their own money for funding because of a disinterested public, worked tirelessly to provide a world for these children.

I knew the Navy had its share of the handicapped, but I had no idea how many. Parents were still reluctant to present them to outsiders. Once again, working with the Red Cross, I offered my plan. Space would be found, volunteers recruited, and psychiatrists, doctors, teachers approached -- anyone who could give their time to train classes of volunteers to work with retarded and handicapped children.

The minister at the Lynnhaven Baptist Church never had a chance. It was a large and wealthy church with many classrooms and when I left his office, two of those classrooms were mine three mornings a week. He must have felt next to God with his generous offer. As far as I was concerned, he was. The word went out to the Red Cross volunteers within the Navy community and they turned up in droves. Every professional I approached was enthusiastic about the idea and offered time and knowledge without charge. We held classes at the Red Cross Headquarters in Norfolk, eighteen miles away, sending out the word through the many commands in the area. On a Monday morning, the church doors were opened to the families and their deeply retarded children.

It was tough. It was very tough. They came in like Alice in Wonderland, unable to believe their eyes. The volunteers went to work and before noon, parents and children alike were responding to the caring women who were having a hard time holding back their tears. After we proved it could be done and done well, the Red Cross asked if they could adopt the program on a national level.

"You bet", I said.

I had one more job with the Red Cross during that long tour of duty. They picked thirteen counties in Virginia and North Carolina and told me to go get their blood. The Tidewater Blood Program was known for its immense area of coverage and extensive benefits. My job was to drive to the various counties, meet with the Red Cross Chairman of Volunteers for that area and see him or her about a Bloodmobile visit.

I stood in bean fields, got chiggers, sat in coal yards, college dean's offices, wherever those Chairmen were and sold them on the idea of saving lives in Vietnam. The military desperately needed blood. It was a bloody war and I had a vested interest. Convincing a field of strawberry pickers in North Carolina to donate their blood required the loan of the town fire truck and with sirens wailing, the firemen drove me to the edge of the field. Standing on the truck in my summer cotton dress, I eyed the curious, but wary faces and said my piece.

"Men, there's a war on and we need your help. We don't want any money – you have little of that as it is. But you were pretty busy last Saturday night in town and because of your knife fights, this county has just about run out of blood. There are some men who wish they could change jobs with you and pick strawberries instead of being shot at. But they can't. Instead, they just bleed until somebody hooks them up and gives them what will keep them alive – your blood."

It worked. They all lined up at the end of the day and stuck out their arms.

Another pilot was down. Another wife was a widow. .

The children were old enough to be aware of all that happened. They enjoyed my story about meeting with the Msattaponi Indians on their reservation, sitting on the ground in their circle and talking about a blood visit. But the newspapers were full of derogatory and negative stories about the war and their father was a part of it. I don't know what private hell they went through at school, but one night when I tiptoed in to cover Jamey, I found her with her father's sweater under her cheek. It was still damp from her tears.

One of my most difficult jobs was discipline. I was the bad guy — the one who always said 'no' and there was no other parent around to soften the order or explain why it must be so. This was my first time around with teenagers and frankly, I was scared to death. I couldn't remember ever being one, and those times bore no resemblance to the ones we were living through. The *'BEATLES'* with their shaggy hair and frantic beat, came down the pike and I reacted like any parent did in the early Sixties. They personified teenage rebellion and I could sense I was losing control. My volunteer jobs always allowed me to be home when they came in from school — I never forgot Jeff's request — but the wear and tear of being a wartime wife, often left me empty and frightened. The children sensed that and were frustrated and frightened, too.

Jim was flying three strikes a day over North Vietnam. Each strike lasted close to two hours, depending on the location of the target. This enemy had SAM missiles that could target a plane and follow it to its destruction. They looked like telephone poles after launch, and it was possible to evade them if the pilot knew how. But the pace of the air battles often kept the pilot's attention and there was no time for evasive action. VA76 lost seven planes and three pilots and its remaining planes suffered severe battle damage.

In October, needing planes desperately, Jim and his boss, the Commander of the Air Group, flew to the Cubi Point Naval Air Station in the Phillipines. The aircraft carrier Oriskany, had suffered a devastating fire, with many of their pilots dying in their rooms of suffocation from the smoke. The final count was forty-four officers and men dead. They no longer had the pilots for their planes and Jim's squadron no longer had the planes for his pilots. Cut and dried – a seemingly cold swap, but war does not progress on sentiment. Nor does it wait.

I picked up the morning Virginia Pilot to see if there was anything on the carriers that were on Yankee Station. It was time for the Enterprise to move back into combat position and that's how we knew where our husbands were. On the back of page one, covering the top half of page two was an article about VA 76 and its leader, Jim Linder. A syndicated media team, visiting aboard the Enterprise had fastened on a particular strike and graphically described the details of the destruction of railroad yards and a bridge -- not just any old bridge, but one the Chinese Communists considered extremely important. The media went on to name Jim as the leader of the strike, where we lived and any other details they could glean from unclassified material through the ship's Information Office.

In short, they set us up. We were now known, which made us a target for any Vietnam war-hater and there were plenty of those to go around. Even the enemy read the syndicated article and responded. In a communiqué from the Chinese Communists, they thanked the American press for supplying them with the name of the man who destroyed their bridge, then added they would be waiting for Commander Linder with special treatment in mind for his future. ;

My coffee was cold and I was colder.

Thus began my own war with the media. They loved Vietnam. Because of relaxed rules from the Department of Defense, they could crawl into foxholes and photograph men dying quickly or by degrees. The more blood, the better. With the advent of tape recorders and video machines, they were able to record for the American public in the comfort of their living rooms, the horrors of war. Stretchers carried maimed men – can't worry about their families seeing them – they were 'just doing their job'. The pictures were invariably followed by editorials condemning our motives in even being there and, by so doing, turning the men who fought in that God forsaken place into criminals.

Patriotism was a little hard to come by in those days.

Patricia Linder

CHAPTER FIFTEEN

The doorbell rang. I looked up from my desk to see four people, standing on the front porch. They were Phillipinos – a man, a very pregnant woman and two children around six and seven. When I opened the door, the man identified himself as a Chief Petty Officer with orders to the Enterprise, off Vietnam. They had just arrived from Pensacola and he was to be on a Navy plane out of Oceana Naval Air Station in one hour and thirty minutes. He said there had been no time to find a place to leave his family, so he brought them to me. I'm still hazy on why me, perhaps because of my work with the Red Cross, but more likely because he was attached to my husband's squadron. Somebody gave him my name and he did the only thing he could think of. There wasn't time to question him – a Navy van waited impatiently at the curb. He placed his hand on the woman's head and said her name, "Felice" then repeated the gesture with each of the children, "Tony" -- "Rachel", bowed politely, shook my hand and was gone. I was the only one remaining who could speak any English.

We whiled away the morning, trying to understand each other. After numerous phone calls to various unbelieving organizations, I was finally instructed to take them to the Navy's housing office where they would be assigned an apartment in enlisted quarters. Moving through the endless wickets took all afternoon with phone calls to my children, explaining where I was and why I wasn't home. Around five, the solid wall of Navy bureaucracy softened enough to place the family before day's end next door to an Eskimo woman who could speak no English, either. The wisdom of that escaped me, but by that time, we were all too tired to question any decision. I drove them to their new home and closed my eyes at the sight of scurrying roaches as we unpacked their suitcases. They stuck to each other, forming one solid person made up of three.

After a trip to the grocery store for the staples that would get them through the night and next day, I called the Red Cross and asked for help. Arrangements were made for a worker to take them through the remaining wickets – school for the children, a hospital check-in visit for the mother-to-be and the necessary network to help this family through the next few months until the husband's return. On Sunday, I picked them up and we all went to church. That, they understood.

Two weeks later, I waited in the lobby of the children's psychiatric hospital to see Tony, the little boy who had climbed the tallest tree he could find and stayed there, rather than go to school. He had his father's bolo knife and according to the interpreter, when his father left for Vietnam, he told his small six-year-old son he must take care of his mother and sister. He was now the man of the house. It was too much responsibility for such a little boy and he simply went haywire. Because of the ship's position on Yankee Station, Tony's father could not come home to help his son.

I was genuinely concerned about Jamey. Her grades were mediocre, she became listless and uninterested. Living with her was like living with a hurt wasp. I knew she missed her father and feared for him and being new in high school only added to her insecurities. Jamey had attended a different school almost every year of her life. During the three-year tour of shore duty, so very long ago, she had kindergarten, first and second grades in the same school. Now, because of "redistricting" within our own community, she was moving again, despite my pleading with the school board. She would automatically lose her place on the coveted drill team. I felt completely helpless to break through her shell. – I couldn't even break through my own.

In Jim's Flight Log Book, dated June 1966, on the fifth day he wrote, "It's all over." The last strike of that eight -month cruise was flown and the men and their ship were ready to return to the United States. The journey from Vietnam to San Francisco took only ten days for the nuclear powered Eenterprise. Jim's squadron flew off the carrier while it was still 200 miles at sea, then began the last long leg of the journey home across the United States to Oceana Naval Air Station in Virginia Beach and his family.

The town decided this was a squadron of heroes so they should have a hero's welcome. The Navy asked that I have the children with me at the field at noon, when the first planes were due. Jim, being the Commanding Officer, would lead them. The mayor was there, three High School bands were vying for everyone's attention and the townspeople turned out to watch. Our little group of women and children – the 'Blythe Spirits of '76', stayed together and tried to keep our excitement under control.

The hours passed, the Mayor left for an important meeting, the band kids had to go home for supper, the townspeople drifted away. No planes. Finally, we were told to go home and wait to be called when they made radio contact with our husbands. Of course we were worried. Where were they? Eight months in Vietnam, flying over unfamiliar enemy territory, yet able to find a carrier in the middle of the South China Sea – at night – where were they?

Around midnight, the phone rang and we were instructed to come to the Base immediately. The planes were on their way in. Jamey insisted we take Charlie, our new Maltese puppy (which Jim knew nothing about). I had broken my toe the day before and was carrying a cane. Jeff curled up in the back seat and dropped off to sleep immediately.

At the field, the tired, broken A-4's limped in. The planes were so shot full of holes, the pilots had put down along the way for repairs – just to get home. Not knowing about the festivities, they used their time on the ground to patch up their planes, instead of making phone calls. We were all a sorry sight. The men were exhausted, unshaven, smelled of jet fuel and there wasn't a white silk scarf among them. It was a good thing the crowd had gone home. But the men were *there*. I watched as Jim wearily pulled his long frame out of the absurdly small plane and dropped to the ground. We waited at the edge of the tarmac for the signal to go to him. What he saw were two children he hardly recognized, a small dog he didn't recognize at all and his wife with a bandaged toe, leaning on a cane. We could have posed for the painting, *The Spirit of '76'.* All we lacked were the piccolo and the drum.

Patricia Linder

CHAPTER SIXTEEN

1967

Hands shaking, I stared at ladies' silk blouses on hangers, knowing something awful was about to descend on me. Leaving early in the morning, we had made the two hundred -mile drive to Washington, D.C. to check on Jim's next set of orders. We would be driving back before dark. He dropped me off at the Marine Exchange, Henderson Hall, then drove on to the Bureau of Personnel. I tried to concentrate on what was in front of me, but my mind was like a kaleidoscope with pictures of the past ten months shifting and sliding.

After his 'heroic' return to Virginia Beach in the dead of night, we all looked forward to having him home with us. There was so much to tell him, so much to share, with words that would tell us of *his* life while away from his family. The children needed him. I needed him.

The seventh grade coach had called the week before with advice that Jeff should not play football, his heart's desire, because he wasn't brawny enough. The man was afraid Jeff would be seriously hurt, considering the size of the other players. It was up to me to deliver the bad news. I was becoming known as the 'no' mother and the bearer of all bad tidings. That kind of news was a guy thing and easier to accept from a father.

But instead of the four of us, it narrowed down once again to three. Soon after his arrival home, he returned to the West Coast to his squadron and transitioned into a different kind of plane. Cross-

131

countries became our way of life with the training more intense because of the war. The months we should have had together, became days or at best, a week or two before the bag was packed and he was on the wing again. I often wondered if I was really married. Sometimes, I felt like a convenience.

Coming out of my reverie, I heard his voice behind me. The Exchange came back into focus.

"Patti, let's go to lunch. I have news." There was suppressed excitement in his words.

Stomach churning, I left the Exchange. What was the matter with me? Why now, did the Chinese Communist message saying they were waiting for his return, come into my thoughts?

The 'news' was he would be returning to Vietnam. He had his Air Group, something he had aspired to throughout his naval career. I was pleased for him to have reached that goal. But at what a price. The odds for his return were getting shorter every day. and my control finally gave way to tears and a hurried march to the ladies' room. On the drive back to Virginia Beach, the silence was palpable. Four hours later as we turned into the driveway, he said, "Will you tell Jamey and Jeff?"

"No, Jim. This one's on you." I couldn't turn my head to look at him.

Jamey listened, knowing the danger he would face once more. As a Navy child, she was aware of the honor of her father's orders, but she would be leaving friends and starting all over once again.

Her only answer was, "Daddy, I give up.'

Shaken, Jim went into Jeff's room and closed the door. His voice was steady and kind, but there was no answering voice from Jeff. Our quiet, introspective boy accepted what had to be and kept his fears to himself. My heart hurt

We listed our White House with a rental agent, packed up the cat and dog and drove the two cars to San Diego. A tornado in Oklahoma took our minds off our problems as we plowed through cloudbursts, floods and the devastation of a countryside.

But uppermost in my mind were teenagers in California in the Sixties. The safety of my husband, I could do nothing about.

California houses are built on the premise that they will either careen down a hill during a landslide, or that the hill will fall on them. Our first house was waiting to be buried under tons of dirt and the hill that could do it was twenty feet from the back door. It went straight up. I began each day, staring at dirt.

To put it kindly, the house was small. By sitting in the wing chair in the living room, I could view every room on its three levels. Good for keeping track of teenagers, but hard on the psyche. It was real togetherness.

The most we saw of Jim was his back as he packed his bag. Air Groups consist of eight or nine squadrons of various types of planes and Jim's command was a split one. Several squadrons were based at Miramar Naval Air Station in San Diego, but his Staff and other squadrons were based in Lemoore, California, a master jet base for the West Coast, just south of Fresno in the San Jaoquin Valley. In short, he had to be in two places at once. Navy wives referred to Lemoore as the 'survival school for dependents', a takeoff on the real survival school our husband pilots were required to attend before going into combat. During his week at that particular prep school, Jim was buried alive with another man on top of him for the better part of an hour – one of the more palatable forms of torture in an otherwise miserable seven days of interrogation methods. It was training for the possibility of being shot down over enemy territory and becoming a prisoner of war.

For the dependents in Lemoore, Quarters were provided on the Base where nearly everyone chose to live. The families melded into one large family, offering strong support for each other. When the reports of downed fliers came in and the Casualty Assistance Officers appeared at the front door with the Chaplain, everyone knew immediately. They closed ranks to help.

San Diego was a different matter. There was no compound. The Air Group wives lived throughout the city. There were no ranks to close. We were on our own in a city known for its dislike of the war.

I enrolled the children in their two schools. At Jamey's high school, the principal met me at the front desk, annoyed that Jamey was entering a month late, despite my explanation.

"She'll have a lot of catching up to do and the teachers here set a high standard for their pupils. You should also know there is a seventy five percent drug usage in the school."

The thought crossed my mind that with those drug figures, who met the 'high standards'?

Jeff's grammar school was no better. We both felt antipathy and disinterest from the seventh grade principal. The drug usage percentage was the same. I went home reeling.

In the wing chair, staring at the dust ruffle on our bed and the fireplace in the downstairs den at the same time, I knew sitting here in this house, waiting for bad news that could now come from every direction, would drive me over the edge. I checked the phone book, called Sharp's Memorial Hospital and asked what was available for a somewhat qualified volunteer. Three days later, after the children had settled into their schools and with Jim in Lemoore, I presented myself to the Clinic for Deaf Children. Working one-on-one, I taught deaf children how to hear. To see the wonder on a child's face when, through amplified sound, they heard music or the human voice for the first time, gave me joy. In those days, I needed all the joy I could find.

At the beginning of the war in Vietnam, President Johnson coined the phrase, "Guns and Butter"; indicating it was quite possible to have a war and at the same time, enjoy prosperity on the home front, thereby guaranteeing election votes. So much for the military. It was a neat little piece of politics, but the phrase diminished what was happening on the other side of the world. The President himself, made the decision to 'engage the guns', without Congressional approval, but the message he gave with the 'butter' was , "Go fight the war, just don't ruffle the feathers of the Great Society on the home front." Bad for elections. The media labeled it 'divisive', accusing the war of creating a split within our own country. Protesting became an art and in some cases, a profession.

The scapegoats were anyone actively engaged in fighting 'that dirty war'. Harvard professor, Timothy Leary unleashed his diatribe on the children, encouraging them to 'kick the Establishment', load up on drugs and have a high old time. "Do your own thing", he told them. It was the 'beat generation'. and California was where the war was. What happened in the Sixties changed our country and our lives forever because the fundamentals began to crumble.

Western seacoast cities were the launching pads for the ships, men and planes, heading across the Pacific Ocean into combat. The concentration of the weapons of war was heaviest in California and that state was more passionate about their hatred for the war than the rest of the country. Our military men became the bad guys with the media feeding on that hatred.

Many of the churches were avidly against the war and one minister, after labeling Jim a 'killer of helpless Vietnamese children' in front of our own children and the congregation, turned up on our doorstep a few months later to see why we were no longer attending his church. Our men were flying combat in Vietnam, and a newly widowed wife had come to my house for comfort and help. When the doorbell rang, I answered it, finding myself face to face with the same minister. He registered shock and confusion, for he recognized me. Stepping through the door, I closed it behind me and spoke softly to him.

"In my house is a young woman whose Navy pilot husband was shot down and killed by one of your 'helpless' North Vietnamese. I would invite you in to meet this new widow, but you are not welcome in my home."

I shut the door. When I turned to look out the window, he was hurrying up the street in the direction of his church. I almost hoped he would find no comfort there.

We moved from the little house to a condominium nearby, keeping the children in their same schools. I no longer stared at the dirt hill every day and hoped the change would have a good effect on my deteriorating disposition.

Making the decision to begin work on my Masters Degree in Special Education at San Diego State University, my days were filled with the Clinic for Deaf Children and school. But the coming months would find me with more serious responsibilities than I thought possible. I was faced with the choice between a graduate degree or doing my job as a Commanding Officer's wife. There was not time for both. The degree became a pearl in my pocket – something to be enjoyed at a later date.

Our children felt the hatred for the war at their schools. Jamey was a beautiful girl with long, blonde hair and a smile that lit up my soul. Coming into a new school from another part of the country, she made few friends. The other girls considered her competition and with a father in Vietnam, she was immediately segregated. At first, we talked of the new problems facing her, but as time passed, she

137

grew silent and reluctant to discuss them. I worried about drugs, but the night of the junior prom, when her date slipped something into her punch, she came home desperately ill. She was allergic to alcohol and drugs. It was then that I realized she had only been trying to protect me, as I tried to protect her.

Jeff made friends more easily. With his shy smile and pewter gray eyes that hinted at a good sense of humor, he marched his new friends through our house and like boys everywhere, left a trail of banana peels and cookie crumbs. He was a good student, with the ability to fit in easily, but his father's erratic schedule left them little time together. Like his sister, he kept his hurts to himself and we struggled on. I could see the changes in both of our children each day as they faced their battles.

CHAPTER SEVENTEEN

October 24ʰ, 1967

Jim's Air Group lost almost an entire squadron. The enemy was ready and waiting, thanks to thorough U.S. newspaper coverage of the coming strike on Phuc Yen Airport, northwest of Hanoi. At the C.O's quarters on Miramar Naval Air Station, I was told that Jim was also down with the other missing pilots, a fact I refused to accept. In following my request for confirmation, they found it was another mistake in communication. Once again, I would be spared the agony of telling our children they had lost their father. But nineteen women's lives were irrevocably changed and it was up to the chaplains, doctors, Casualty Assistance Officers and me to tell them. That night is permanently engraved on my memory. In contrast to the warm San Diego darkness, was the cold finality of the messages we gave to each wife. No hysterics, no anger – just the acceptance by women who had already come to terms with the possibility. One young wife was pregnant with her first child. She laid her hand on the baby she carried as if to shield it from reality. There would be many tears, but these women would protect each other, saving their grief for themselves.

A week later, on a soft October afternoon, my soul ran out of gas. My soul and every word of consolation or comfort I had ever learned. They were spent – used up, and so was I.

The initial shock of the news was wearing off. As we sat together, I saw fear, anger, bewilderment and agony as these wives realized how different their lives were to become. These were proud women who loved their husbands enough to accept the dangers they faced in their daily lives in spite of their country's dislike of this unpopular war.

Guilt rode me because of the mistaken report of Jim's death. He was still alive. As I left the wives, to be with the young woman carrying her first child, I knew I had no more words of comfort left.

Driving down the Mission Valley freeway in the noon sun, I looked up and to my right. A convent stood regally on one of the high hills above the valley below. Unconsciously, I turned off the freeway and found my way to its front door where, gliding noiselessly to my side, the Sisters welcomed me in as I introduced myself.

"Patricia, how may we help you?"

I looked into a benign face with smiling eyes. Then I told my story of the downed flyers, their wives and children and what had become an impossible task that lay ahead of me on this afternoon.

At last, my tears came as their smiling eyes turned to ones of sympathy and a hand touched my arm. The good sisters were, for a moment unsure of what to do next. I was stunned to think my control, so carefully guarded had given away in front of strangers.

These wise sisters sensed that underneath the tears lay a deep and consuming anger. It too, had been held in check for a time longer than I could remember. They questioned me gently, giving me time to sort out what had happened in my mind. I found them all around me, like dark butterflies. As with my daughter, their luminous faces were shadowed with sadness.

"My dear, we can't bring them back, but we can say a mass for each man."

"But sister, does it matter that some of them are of a different faith?"

"No, Patricia. With this, we are all together in one faith – our faith in God."

"Sister, what do I do next?" I felt inadequate, unknowing.

"Can you provide us with the names of the men and their wives?" One of the sisters had found paper and pencil and I was gently guided to a table and chair in a spartan office. I let the words come, amazed I could recall each man and his wife. The children's names eluded me however, so I simply noted which ones had families.

They left me alone, knowing the quiet of the sunny office would help me remember.

When I turned to go, there was not a doubt in my mind that these soft-voiced sisters would speak their prayers and make a difference.

Later that afternoon, knowing that a mass would be said for her husband, the young, pregnant wife gave free rein to her tears and I sensed she was relieved and comforted.

A VALENTINE FROM A SIX YEAR OLD SON TO HIS
PILOT FATHER, ABOARD THE U.S.S. ENTERPRIS:
Happy Valentine's Day, Daddy
I hope you come home alive.
Bobbie

Patricia Linder

CHAPTER EIGHTEEN

Those who lived, became Prisoners of War. As the media reported their names, the wives received phone calls filled with hatred and condemnation. One wife called me in the middle of the night with the news that the Kremlin in Moscow had contacted her by phone for information on her missing- in- action husband. I suspected a crank call hut immediately got in touch with our caring friend in Communications. He took it from there.

It was no crank call. Using a woman's grief, they preyed on her for information.

The children survived with scars on their hearts. Jeffrey was growing into a tall, slim boy with a sensitive face and sad eyes. Jamey was withdrawing more every day. I seldom saw her smile. There was no good news – no happiness or joy. We made it from day to day, dealing with whatever we had to, talking as little as possible about the war. Our defenses were up. They had to be. I often felt deprived of the warmth of a mother's love for her children. The love was always there, but any chink in the armor meant collapse. I felt like a badly cracked dam.

We did things together. San Diego offered the beach, the zoo, Sea World and movies. But the children were teenagers and wanted lives of their own. By choice, neither was interested or involved in school activities due to the lateness of their registration and we all floated. At the library one day, I searched the section on teenagers, hoping to find something that would give me some guidelines. This was my first

143

time around as a parent of that particular age child and without a husband to help, I was floundering. The title on the book was, *Years of Horror*. Thinking it had been misplaced in that section, I took it to the librarian.

"Oh no, it's not out of place. It belongs right where you found it." She smiled sympathetically and I sensed from the expression on her face that she had the same problems I did.

Because some of the squadrons in Jim's Air Group were stationed in Lemoore, we made the long, full day's drive to meet with the wives who had lost their husbands during the Phuc Yen strike. We stayed with an old and dear friend whose husband was also on the combat line but on a different ship. Martha had always had a deep sense of God in her life and she told me that weekend as we talked about surviving, "I pray to make it to noon. Then I pray to make it to night." Her faith served her well as she shared with the other wives. They leaned on her for strength. She never failed them.

As Christmas approached, my parents invited us down to Guadalajara, Mexico to spend the holiday with them. Because of my father's heart trouble, they drove to Mexico every year, took an apartment and stayed until spring to avoid the long, cold Iowa winters. Through the years they had always found time to visit us, sometimes baby-sitting so Jim and I could be alone together, but usually, just to be family again. They understood the life we lived only by being with us. Spending Christmas with them was a godsend, not only for the children, but for their mother, too.

The travel office reported the runways were crumbling in Guadalajara, but we needed time away from the stress in our lives and, taking the chance of ending up in an airport ditch was worth it. Different sights and different sounds. My mother the artist, had made friends with a bullfighter – one of Mexico's finest – and she painted the handsome, young toreador often. The children who clustered around mother as she strolled the streets, received small bars of soap along with the saved-up change she gave them. With her plump, Iowa figure and snowy hair, she moved among them, brown eyes smiling. They called her 'Honey', just as we did and her family grew with every day. We had dropped into a different world.

It was difficult to return to the other. The Mexican people charmed us with their wide smiles and dark eyes. The bright colors of the city belied the slumbering countryside. The hills had a look of wildness to them, as though no one had ever set foot on them before. It was easy to imagine Pancho Villa or Zapata hiding among the dusty rocks. But it was time -- school would resume in a few days. For safety's sake, we had to get out before those runways completely crumbled away.

Together, my father and I walked the streets one last time. I took the arm of this tall, gentle man with the warm smile and understanding eyes. My thoughts drifted back to my own years as a teenager in the happy, carefree busyness so naturally taken for granted. How different from my own children's lives. I felt a pang of guilt that they could not know the same secure contentment that was mine at their age.

145

His, steady voice gentled me as he said, "Patti, it's been a bad time, hasn't it? I can see it on your face and in your eyes. I know Jim's all right or you would have told us, but when you first arrived, you looked heartsick."

Good term – heartsick. It was a perfect description of my state of mind. I had always shielded my family from the less palatable parts of our lives, but my father, the canny Scot, knew when things were wrong. Briefly, I told him of the past few weeks and what was yet to come. Listening quietly, he shook his head, pulled me to him and said, "Stay strong, daughter. You can do it."

The beat of the drum continued on into spring. More men down, not just from our ship, but all the ships on Yankee Station. More widows and more women who would wait seven years to see their husbands again, if they survived the POW camps. One of our Air Wing wives had an alcohol problem that we had tried to deal with together. On a quiet morning when I opened the door to retrieve the newspaper, I found her unconscious on the front porch. Unable to live with the almost daily destruction of pilots and the possibility of losing her own husband, she had made a failed attempt at suicide. The children helped me as I pulled her into the house and checked to see if she was still alive. Their faces were closed. They fixed their own breakfasts, then silently left for school. I don't know whom I felt sorriest for. The fragile woman survived and her frantic mistake remained unknown to all but my family.

It was the era of runaways, and who could blame them? A lousy war, the lure of the 'flower children', Timothy Leary's drug- induced promises, and San Francisco's Haight Ashbury neighborhood that became the gathering place for the sad-eyed, hard-faced teenagers' dreary lives, saturated television as the media sniffed tragedy. Pepsi Cola's advertisement of a girl, astride a horse, hair flying in the wind, as they pounded through the Pacific surf, was certainly more exciting than homework. So they bundled up as little as possible of the 'Establishment', positioned themselves along the roadsides, thumbs out, heading north or east or south to the land of pot and honey. They lived in communes, ate what everybody else ate, if there was anything *to* eat and after the first excitement of being 'free' and on their own, tried not to notice the lonely fear that crawled around in the backs of their minds. Some stayed to become professional drop-outs, some were never heard from again, except by the California police who logged them in and tried to find the parents to send either the teenager or his death notice to.

The telephone became my enemy. Each time it shrilled, I expected the worst.

On a Saturday afternoon, one of the squadron wives called. She sounded far away, breathless and terrified.

"Pat, you've got to help me get word to my husband on the ship. The San Francisco police just called and they want Sarah's dental records." Her voice strangled. "They have a body that might be our daughter's. It matches her description." She wept.

147

I promised to put the wheels in motion. Hanging up, I shook my fist at God and voiced that age-old question, "Why?"

The Sixties' main product was casualties – wartime and teenage.

When the ships went off the combat line on Yankee Station, they usually steamed into Hong Kong because it was the closest liberty port. Since the end of World War II, Japan refused entry to any nuclear vessel, so often, Hong Kong was the only place available for the men to leave their ship. Combat on Yankee Station could last as long as a month with the pilots flying three to four strikes a day. A few wives saved their money and flew to that exotic city, knowing full well their husbands might be there only two or three days, but willing to make the long trip if it meant time together. It didn't always work. One carrier arrived, only to receive orders to report back on line immediately. A very disappointed wife returned to San Diego after only glimpsing her husband as he stood on the quarterdeck of the ship, while she waited on the pier.

My own husband had made it crystal clear that "This is war and it's no place for a woman." With teenagers and Air Group responsibilities, I tended to agree with him, although the desire to just run away from it all crept into my thoughts from time to time.

The realities of flying combat strikes were hard ones. Because of the nature of the war, the Administration and the Defense Department labeled it a 'limited war' or 'conflict' -- a guarantee of defeat, thereby reducing it in importance to the American public The Vietnam War became the longest one in our country's history. It lasted from 1964 to 1975, when the prisoners of war were returned. Eleven deadly years.

. The media reported an uncomfortable twist. In their sleuthing for news, they discovered that target decisions, instead of being made by on-scene commanders in the war area, were coming from the Oval Office in the White House and the Defense Department, half a world away. One story graphically told of pilots in their planes on the flight deck, engines going, waiting for their target designation from Washington D.C. It was even suggested that because of that wait, men took off with less than enough fuel to return to the carrier. Another story told of targets being nothing more than bomb craters from previous strikes. Either way, men were shot down or didn't make it back.

I was grateful to the media for their reporting. For once, they were on our side, but it was hard not to become cynical and angry. These were our husbands. It mattered to us the degree of danger they were in, especially when their own country put them there. Ask the men and they would say, "It's our job."

Luckily, nobody asked us.

But underneath, many of the men questioned the orders that put them in their planes and sent them out to destroy a faceless enemy. They had been trained to obey and the President was their Commander in Chief. His orders were followed to the letter, but confidence in his judgement and that of the Secretary of Defense was lacking.

149

In the words of one pilot – a friend, on home rotation from Vietnam, "It's a cockamamey war."

While sitting at lunch one day with the wife of another Air Group Commander, she looked me straight in the eye and said, "What am I going to tell our two sons when they grow up and ask why their father went to Vietnam?"

"Mickey, tell them he made a commitment to serve his country and because he is a man of honor, he did what his country demanded of him."

One July morning, I stood outside my door, transfixed, staring at the three-inch headline in the San Diego Union newspaper:

<u>FORRESTAL ON FIRE!</u>

My eyes traveled down to the story below the headline. The aircraft carrier, Forrestal had sustained a cataclysmic event when rockets and bombs ignited on its flight deck. The ship lay dead in the water and vulnerable on Yankee Station off North Vietnam. The date was July 29th, 1967. Most of the eighteen and nineteen year-olds who worked the flight deck, were killed as they struggled to contain the fires set off by 150 tons of bombs and rockets. An old World War II, 'cost effective' thin-skinned rocket had started it.

The pictures were graphic and devastating. My hands were shaking when I heard the sing-song voice of my next-door neighbor, as she peered at the same picture on her paper. She had often needled me about Jim's participation in the war. I avoided her as much as possible, but this morning found us outside at the same time. Bad timing.

She snickered when she asked, "What's a Forrestal?"

I seethed at the off hand, flippant question. "Well Goldie, it's an aircraft carrier with five thousand American men on it and at the moment, it's on fire and burning in the South China Seas. If you look closely, you can even see several of those men dead on the deck." I was beyond polite.

Goldie merely said, "Ugh" , then turned to go inside, making it perfectly clear she wasn't interested.

There was to be a future irony to the Forrestal story. In just six years, my husband would become its Commanding Officer.

1968

After eight months, when the Coral Sea returned to the United States, San Francisco pulled out all the stops. Because the city had adopted the ship as its own, the festivities were spectacular. Jim with his squadrons from San Diego, flew into Miramar ahead of the ship's return as the families gathered at the airfield to welcome their men back. The fear and sadness I had grown accustomed to seeing on their faces were gone, replaced by the almost hysterical joy they felt to see their men. Expressions of their love would come later in the private quiet of their homes. Today, it was relief and the excitement of knowing the men were alive. One or two had the haunted look of women who could take no more. Possibly, their first evening with their husbands would be spent exploring alternatives to this way of life. Marriages often experienced the greatest threat at the end of a combat cruise. If the man could not give up his commitment and the wife could no longer live the life, the marriage ended. I had seen it happen before.

My own feelings were mixed. I thanked God – the same one I had shaken my fist at – that Jim had survived. But I could see the hardness in his face and knew he was still on Yankee Station, waiting for planes that would never come back. I seldom had his complete attention and this day was no exception. But he *needed* us and the arms that hugged him – Jamey's, Jeff's and mine – conveyed only love and joy. The hard lines softened.

On the low, flat roof of the Operations building, a group of women sat on folding chairs. They were the wives of the men who did not come back. Their husbands were either dead, missing in action or prisoners of war. They had made their own arrangements, not wanting to spoil the day for the women who now held their husbands in their arms.

One of them told me, as Jim spoke with each wife, "I knew if I didn't see his plane land and taxi into its place, he was truly gone."

We made the long drive the next morning to San Francisco to greet the battle-weary Coral Sea as she slowly nosed into her berth. A celebration rivaling any New Years Eve gala told the crew lining the decks how glad the city was to have them home. Of course the protestors from Berkeley University were there, but nothing could dim the happiness of families together again.

The beginning of it all. Iowa, 1949

Jim with camera.

Sqdn. VF112   Korea

153

Jamey, our daughter

Jeffrey, our son

Jim as an A-4 attack pilot – Korea

USS Phillipine Sea – Korea

The 'People Ship' USS Forrestal and its Skipper.

Tunisian President Bourgiba decorating Jim with VADM 'Fox' Turner, attending

A Linder takeoff in an F-4 Phantomj

Change of Command -- Forrestal. Jim becomes an Admiral

Pat and an old ruin Italy

USS Forrestal at sea. *Mediterranean*

Jim reviewing the troops during typhoon

Taipei, Taiwan

Pat -- Quarters A,
Taipei, Taiwan

The Admiral

His Navy wife

CHAPTER NINETEEN

May, 1968

A certain numbness settled on me. The crawling fear I had felt for so long receded to the back labyrinth of my tired mind and left me punchy. The frantic, unrestrained plethora of emotions that accompanied the return of the ship had a carnival quality and I couldn't find my place in the festivities. My greatest desire was for a quiet time to sort it all out, putting memories away until there was room and acceptance for what was ahead.

The young wives' exuberance would carry them through to the next challenge, which for many, would be another Vietnam tour of duty. My limitations were by now, well known to me, having met my blooding ground. The cold, unrelenting demands of a government had invaded my family and left permanent scars. I was tired to the death of the politics of patriotism.

Jamey had withdrawn to the point of estrangement. She adamantly refused to consider college, saying only that what she truly wanted was to be married and have her own family. No argument would shake her resolve. She had met a boy and was determined to share the rest of her life with him. We were equally determined she would not.

The stand down period for the Air Group came to an end as Jim learned the need for what they called 'cannibalizing'. When a plane crashed anywhere in the U.S., pilots flew to the sight to pick it clean of useable parts.

"Patti, I'll be gone for a few days. There's a plane that's crashed in Nevada and we have to go see about parts." Would the grimness ever leave his face? Would I ever see him smile again?

"Parts? A crashed plane? Is it something you can talk about?" I had not asked for information about anything after his return. In time, he would talk about the cruise. Maybe not. Losing men must have been a living hell and until he *needed* to let it out, I would respect his silences.

Wearily he said, "The DOD (Department of Defense) had the dies for the spare parts of our older planes scrapped when the newer planes came out. It was more 'cost effective'. Trouble is, we're still flying the older models and when a plane crashes anywhere in the country, we have to fly in for a shot at retrieving parts we can use to keep our planes flying."

Just back from Vienam, Jim's pilots scrambled to keep their planes in the air and if it meant picking over the corpse of a crashed plane in Missouri or Nevada, they did it.

"Fly gently, dear. And come home as soon as you can." I was past being shocked or horrified at anything.

Nothing made sense anymore. There was only the reality that men died needlessly, serving their country.

Jim's orders were cut, with the Change of Command scheduled to be held in Lemoore. Washington duty loomed on the horizon. For me it would be the chance to fade back into the woodwork. I didn't know how Jim felt.

Didn't really care at that point.

Lemoore

Instead of the standard ceremony in the hangar, Jim's Change of Command was held next to a runway. My numbed thoughts didn't register the unusual location, so intent was I on keeping myself together through yet, one more official function. The morning wore on with speeches, awards and commendations. The left side of Jim's uniform was steadily filling with medals. I listened to the names of men who, with valor and courage, gave everything they had but didn't make it back. As the descriptions of their deeds were read, I imagined what *they* had seen; the barrages of anti-aircraft fires, SAM missiles coming at them with frightening speed as they dodged enemy aircraft interceptors during the gut-wrenching intensity of their mission. Then nothing.

The wives rose to receive their husband's medals.

I heard my name called and was gently propelled out of my chair to the podium where a medal was pinned on my dress. Someone decided I had earned more than a pat on the back, so a medal was struck. I could feel tears gathering. Sympathy and recognition meant only loss of control to me and this was not the place. Thank God for dark glasses.

On the empty runway sat a plane, propeller stationary. It was an AD Skyraider -- an A-1 medium attack bomber. In Vietnam, besides flying medium to low level bombing runs, the AD escorted helicopters during overland rescue operations. Propeller powered, without the advantage of a jet's speed, the plane with its pilot was a sitting duck. On this June morning, the single Skyraider, representing its squadron, looked more like a small lonely icon.

That one remaining Navy AD squadron had been in Jim's Air Group aboard the Coral Sea, but today VA-25, known as 'The Fist of the Fleet' would be decommissioned. This plane would not be going back into battle for the Navy. Instead, it was destined for a museum.

As I watched, a tall, slim, handsome young pilot in his flight suit, walked across the empty tarmac, turned, saluted and with white silk scarf lifting gently in the breeze, climbed into his plane. He took off, circled the field once and flew out of sight. A few moments later, as we heard its engines, the A-1 came back into view. The pilot had rendezvoused with an F-8 Crusader super sonic jet and together, they made ready for the final pass over the field. Flying at full speed, the A-1 led, with the Crusader, wheels down, wing up, following in its wake. The jet struggled to go slowly enough to let the A-1 take the lead. It was a perfect example of the affection and respect pilots have for each other and the planes that respond to their touch.

There wasn't a dry eye in the house.

Mt. Pleasant, Iowa, June 1968

My father looked fragile. Stopping by to see my family on our journey back to Washington, I felt a slight trembling in his shoulders as we held onto each other. The wisdom was still in his eyes and noticing Jamey's on-going silences and lack of interest in her appearance, he knew my challenges were not over.

Putting his cheek on my hair, he said, "Patti, troubles with your children are the hardest to bear. Your mother and I know all about that. But remember, the way they were before these difficult times, will be what they become when they're grown."

'These difficult times' were the sixties and the experience he spoke from was the Great Depression. With two obstreperous teenage boys to put through college, in those lean years, my parents had struggled – and won.

Our days together were happy ones, and we left with the gentling that comes from family love.

I knew I would lose him soon.

In the weeks that followed, Jamey's young man from California would come striding up the front walk after riding a bus and hitchhiking from San Diego to Washington, D.C. to claim the girl he wanted to spend his life with. No amount of reasoning would budge their determination. She was just eighteen when they left us and married, leaving us bereft and frightened for her safety and happiness. (As I write this, their marriage has lasted thirty-two years with children and grandchildren of their own, proving how wrong we were after all.).

Soon after Jamey left, my father died. Wanting only to curl up and make the world go away, I mourned, finally giving myself time to sort through the lightning strikes that seemed never to end.

Jeff, who had weathered the storm better than the rest of us, or at least, had covered his pain well, looked forward to spending the next three years in the same high school with graduation at the end of it.

There was a steadiness about the boy that I had leaned on often. With his father home once again, his sparkle returned and life went on.

My mother came for a time of healing after Dad's death and announced at dinner one evening that she was sending Jeff to Europe in the summer. A study group of young students had formed up and with their chaperones, would tour Spain, France and England. We were delighted, but knowing my mother, not too surprised. She was an astute observer of people and had sensed Jeff's pain during the past two years when most of our attention had been on his sister.

The trip was highly successful. Cleaning his desk one day after his return, I noticed a photograph of our son in a bullring with only a cape in his hand, facing a young bull. When Jeff swung in from school, I had to hear the rest of the story.

"Hey, sweetie, look what I found on top of your desk today when I dusted. I nearly had a heart attack when I looked at it. Was this part of the curriculum? The brochure didn't say anything about a bullfight."

He strung his long length across the bed as he peeled the eternal banana while the family Siamese cat staked out her territory on his chest. "Oh yeah. I forgot I still had it. Pretty neat day. We went out to this bull farm and the owner let me take the cape and go into the ring."

"I can see that. Have any trouble getting out of the ring?"

I had been to bullfights in Mexico and knew there came that moment when the best thing to do was cut and run.

"Not much. The bull chased me around for awhile and I flapped the cape at him, but he finally lost interest. No big deal."

"So you didn't get the ears and the tail. Pity."

He grinned and so did I. We moved up a notch to Paris.

"What did you think of the awful Eiffel tower?"

"Well, actually Mom, I didn't get too good a look. My buddy on the trip had an uncle living on the Left Bank and we split from the bunch and spent the week over there."

I resisted looking heavenward for help. "See much of that part of Paris?"

"Yeah, we sure did. He'd lived there since he was in High School and knew all the best places."

To my credit, I did not ask the best places for what. "Good food?"

"Oh yeah, the food was great, too."

Moving right along to England, I silently labeled myself a coward and asked what they did in London.

"Got lost on the subway. We spent most of one day, going from one end of London to the other."

"Underground?"

"Yeah, but we made up for it the rest of the week."

In deference to my nervous system that was still in a somewhat shaky state, I assumed the rest of his time in England was spent in museums and cathedrals. I didn't ask, he didn't offer. After all, it was a fait accompli. He was happy and the twinkle was back in his eyes.

169

Patricia Linder

Our house in Washington went together faster than I had thought. There was too much time to stand at the window and observe the leaves on the trees. A good friend mentioned they needed volunteers to work on Capitol Hill for an organization called, *HEROES*, an acronym for 'Help Elect Republican Office Holders '. I applied, made the list, then proceeded with the very important work of licking stamps, envelopes and anything else that needed to go out to a constituent. Being able to type helped. We rotated around the halls of Congress (on the House side) and I began to learn.

The language, to begin with. To tell the constituent on the other end of the telephone the Congressman was on 'The Floor', took some doing. Of course everyone knew it was the Floor of the House of Representatives, but for a fledgling it could mean anything from too many martinis at lunch, or the man was in the throes of a heart attack. Neither option was unrealistic.

Breaking all the rules, I said yes to a Congressman's invitation to join his Staff. The *HEROES* were volunteers only, but having had the taste of the power of Congress, licking stamps didn't cut it. This was a world to be learned about and the sponge I called my mind, soaked it up.

Roger Zion was a Republican Congressman from Indiana, highly thought of and astute in his profession. He preferred a small staff of six -- and one, the receptionist, left to begin a new career as a housewife. I had no honed skills other than a monumental patience and an ability to meet people, so my receptionist's desk was first on

170

the left of the big room with the soaring ceiling. It was also directly in the Congressman's line of sight.

I dealt with visiting constituents from the Congressman's 13th District; respectful Boy Scouts, Girl Scouts, members of other Staffs, lost or confused constituents of other districts, smiling lobbyists, steely-eyed union leaders -- anyone who came through the tall door. After the thirty minutes it took me to figure out how to turn on the typewriter, I typed anything that came across my desk. Each afternoon at three, I straightened my desk, turned off the typewriter and made the long drive home, in time for Jeff's arrival from school.

CHAPTER TWENTY

The next two years were pure therapy for me with new faces, laughter, exciting moments and a different viewpoint on history. The Staff became like a family and was endlessly tolerant of the mistakes I made. Congressman Zion became 'Roger', as he was to everyone, making me feel at ease in this strange, new world.

But the war, like moving mist, slipped across our busy lives. Jim came home from his office in the Bureau of Personnel one evening. He was a 'detailer', the man who chooses other men's next tour of duty. It was not a job that came with a lot of friends. Carelessly, he tossed a slim volume covered with navy blue silk onto the chair.

"Interesting day." He recounted a couple of incidents I found only mildly of interest.

"And……..?"

"They gave me the Navy Cross this afternoon."

I was stunned. That medal was the highest form of recognition the Navy bestows, second only to the Congressional Medal of Honor. The only thing lacking in his announcement was 'oh, by the way'. I felt the flash of pride, the thrill of his achievement and the slight for not being invited to see my husband receive it. Washington Navy was quite different from the operational Navy we had just come from.

The slim volume contained the description of the strike and battle that had won him this honor. As I read it, my hands turned damp with belated fear for his life.

"Was there a ceremony?"

"No, Admiral Duncan pinned it on me in his office."

Thanks a lot, Admiral Duncan. It would have been nice.

1969

On Capitol Hill, my days became hectic. Events occurred at lightning speed, the pace of conversation was frenetic, sentences seldom finished. It was the era of the mini skirt with secretaries competing to see whose could be the shortest. Parking in the Longworth garage required an escalator ride to the first floor and that meant a gaggle of men at the bottom, ushering cute young things onto the moving stairway. Gallantry, it was not. But those same men striding the halls of Congress did smile a lot.

With my skirt closer to my knees than most, I exited the elevator, rounded the corner and bumped solidly into Bella Abzug, or Bella the Bull, the name given her by the other Members.. Bella was a Congresswoman who could be identified by her tank-like build and the ubiquitous hat that never left her head, even on the floor of the House. But one didn't need to see Bella, to know she was in the vicinity. Bella the Bull used four letter words that only sailors and longshoremen knew and she used them as often as possible. No person, no place was sacred, including the floor of the House of Representatives. When we collided, it was like hitting a solid brick wall that swore. Flat on the marble floor, I noticed her hat was still firmly in place..

Bella had other talents. When the District police rounded up the peaceniks and ushered them into Kennedy stadium for an overnight cool down, Bella appeared with armloads of toilet paper, pitching them over the fence to the grimy crowd. Always a champion of the 'oppressed', she was a self-avowed card-carrying Communist. This merely confirmed the fact that in this country, anybody can be anything they desire and still be elected to Congress.

On the other side of the coin was the man I worked for: Eagle Scout, Naval officer in the Pacific, successful business man, family man, author, member of Committees, and who, as a Republican had been elected to Congress four times out of a Democratic district. He was a man for all seasons. Probably one of the wittiest men in Congress, his wide smile always drew a responding one. We, his Staff, were inordinately proud of him. There was an aura that followed these public servants; they stood out in a crowd. On their home turf in the marble halls, they had celebrity status and contrary to my previously pedestrian assessment, they earned it.

I looked up from the birthday letter I was typing to a constituent to find the roving Washington correspondent, Arlo Wagner standing by my desk. Periodically, he dropped by for any interesting news from the Congressman's office to go into one of the many newspapers that cover Congressional business.

In our idle conversation, we discovered we were both from Iowa, growing up in towns just a few miles apart. Since I was new to the job, he asked the usual questions. When he discovered I was a Navy wife, he asked about Vietnam. I told him. After ten minutes, he moved on with the promise he would return when we could both talk without so many interruptions. He was particularly interested in the Prisoners of War.

I nodded and was about to resume my typing, when I noticed Roger at his desk, watching me. He crooked his index finger, giving me the 'in here, young lady' look. Thinking I had broken some cardinal rule, I walked into his office, prepared for a lecture, but he said, "Tell me about the Prisoners of War. I overheard the conversation out there and I think you know something I need to know."

Briefly, and with relief at not being scolded, I told him essentially what had just passed between the reporter and me. He asked many questions, but my Navy training compelled me to call Jim in his office in the Pentagon before answering all of them. Jim gave me carte blanche to tell the truth so I told the story of the Missing in Action and Prisoners of War. When I finished, Roger sat lost in thought. Finally, he raised his head and looked at me.

"Pat, this office is going to become the nerve center for Capitol Hill on the issue of these men. I have only one man in my district who is missing in action, but numbers don't matter. We're going to make a difference."

Make a difference, he did. Working together, and with his sponsorship, we drafted the "National Week of Concern for Prisoners of War/Missing in Action". It was a Joint House/Senate Resolution, signed by President Nixon. It urged Americans to write to the Delegate General of North Vietnam in Paris demanding that he conform to the provisions of the Geneva conventions, as it applied to POW/MIA's.

Roger also wrote a letter to Pham Van Dong, the premier of the Democratic Republic of Vietnam. He expressed the outrage of the entire Congress at the inhuman treatment of these men by the North Vietnamese and Viet Cong, by denying the Red Cross access to them, the lack of medical care and no exchange of mail.

Walking the letter around the House corridors, I explained to four hundred and twenty-eight Congressmen what I held in my hand and asked for their signatures. With the exception of twenty-one Democrats and two Republicans, every member signed. H.R.Gross of Iowa, an arch conservative took offense at the salutation of the letter that referred to the enemy as 'Your Excellency'. Had it said 'You S.O.B.', he would have signed.

As I neared the office of a California congressman, I saw the American flag, upside down, puddled on the marble hall floor. Inside his front office were pictures of the Prisoners of War as we had seen them in newspapers and on television newscasts. The pictures were enlarged, framed and hung around the room with a sign that said, 'They are getting what they deserve.' I left the office without bothering to explain my reason for being there.

It was during this time that more bad guys surfaced. Jane Fonda, Ramsey Clark, the Attorney General under the Johnson administration and George McGovern were three Americans the service men in Vietnam heartily disliked. Fonda made a trip to North Vietnam, perched on an anti-aircraft gun and referring to US Navy and Air

Force pilots, said, "I wish I had one of those blue-eyed murderers in my sight." a statement she has never lived down.

In his book, *The Hallowed Howls of Congress*, Congressmanj Zion recounts his experiences with these 'patriots'.

While I was trying to put pressure on the Vietnamese, Jane Fonda and Ramsey Clark were in Southeast Asia trying to get our fighting men to quit. Among other expressions, Fonda said that we should get on our knees and pray for a communist victory.

On the House floor, Father Bob Drinan, a member from Massachusetts, was a spokesman for her and her point of view. I once asked him, in a debate on funding for the House Committee on Internal Security, if we would be permitted to pray if we had a communist victory in this country.

The committee was holding hearings on subversive organizations. I tried to subpoena both Fonda and Clark and charge them with treason. The majority members of the committee didn't go along but they did ask Clark to come before us..................

We showed letters from subversive organizations that cited Clark's work on their behalf and asked him if he was a member of these communist-front groups. He refused to explain his association with them.

On the floor below the Capitol Rotunda, a static display of the bamboo cages with the forms of starving, nearly naked American pilots squatting in the straw, clearly showed the type of treatment these men received, once they were captured. It was graphic and extremely realistic. I lingered for a while to watch the faces as people wandered through the room. Many passed by quickly, averting their eyes, unwilling to address one of the harsher aspects of the war. A little girl around eight, looked at the cage for a long time, then leaving her mother's hand, slowly walked to the display and placed her fingers on the bamboo. Probably her father. I hope never to see such sadness on an eight-year old face again.

Roger waited three weeks for an answer to the letter and when none came, decided at his own expense, to hand -carry the petition with the signatures of the Congress of the United States to the North Vietnamese Legation in Paris. He had written to many of the European Parliaments, explaining his actions, thereby giving them a view of the brutal treatment and torture the North Vietnamese used on their prisoners. Sacks of mail, a result of our letter writing campaign during POW/MIA week were delivered to the Legation's doorstep in Paris. In the opinion of the international community, North Vietnam deserved and got a black eye.

In Paris, the Congressman would be on his own, with no help from our government.

Knowing there were many POW wives already in Paris, hoping for word from the Legation about their husbands, I suggested Roger hold a press conference together with these women to put pressure on Mai Van Bo, the delegate general. After three days, it worked. Congressman Zion was allowed into the Mission building, placed on a chair in the middle of a small room where, after a lengthy wait, he met and engaged in talk with General Van Bo for one hour and forty-five minutes.

"They put me directly in front of a large portrait of Ho Chi Min and looking up at the picture, something went into my eye. Whatever it was, lodged under my contact and with no idea when someone would come in, I was afraid to take out my contact, so I went through the interview with tears running down my cheek." Whatever they thought, it worked.

As he was shown to the door, our signed petition was placed on a table. A metal canister was slipped under his arm – a canister that, although he didn't know it at the time, contained a film of the POWs at a 'Christmas party' -- the first of its kind to ever be released. Later that day, when he saw the film at the US Embassy, he could see how gaunt, hungry and angry the men looked. The staging of the event was crude and obvious. But the countless sacks of anti-Vietnam mail had accomplished what we hoped for.

When the Congressman returned from Paris and recounted his experiences, I felt the thrill of pride at what he was able to do. Wives of the POWs were brought to Washington to view the film and hopefully, identify their husbands, knowing for the first time that they were alive. Copies were made and sent to military bases around the world. Seeing the physical condition of the Prisoners was devastating, but from that time on, things changed and improved for the men.

For some unexplained reason, the North Vietnamese sent home one of the POWs. He was a young pilot in Jim's Air Group when he was shot down. Badly injured, he was confronted in New York by a female peacenik who told him what a criminal he was as he changed planes for Washington, D.C. I knew his wife Jan, and asked her to stay with us when she came to meet him at Andrews Air Force Base.

Close to tears, Jan came into the kitchen as I put the coffeepot on for breakfast.

"Pat, I don't know what to do. I've left my Navy wings at home. When the word came that Ken was coming back, I forgot everything but just getting here. I know he would want to see them on my blouse." She was a fragile girl, still in here twenties and the strain of the past years drew lines on her face that shouldn't have been there. It was always the raw pain in the eyes of these women that left me hurting.

I guided her back to our bedroom, opened the drawer and handed her my wings.

That night, Jan and her husband came back for dinner before the medics whisked him away to Bethesda hospital. The black official car waited at the curb.

At the table, Jan sat next to this skeletal-thin boy whose whole body shook as if from electric shocks. His right arm was badly broken when he crashed and the Viet Cong ignored his injuries. When they finally operated, they broke it again, cut out the misshapen bone and strung it back together with twine. The arm dangled uselessly. He couldn't cut his food.

181

Jan cared for him as she would for a child and, as if in apology for his helplessness, he smiled a crooked smile and said, "I'm glad we don't have pumpkin soup or rice tonight."

Three days later, Jan called from Bethesda where they had taken them both after our brief time together. She told of his excellent care, the round-the-clock attention, then guardedly said, "But I don't know what to do. Pat, they won't let me near him. They have him in a room and I'm only allowed to look at him for a few minutes a day. It's driving both of us crazy." Her voice shook with anger and frustration.

Calling on every female instinct I had, I said, "Jan, is there any piece of furniture in Ken's room that you can move?"

"I don't know. The dresser, maybe. It's not a big one and there's nothing in it."

"Then move it to cover the door. You two need each other and the Navy is not known for understanding a woman's needs."

There were times when I wanted to wring the Navy's neck. Collectively.

The Navy Ball is an annual event in Washington, D.C. Jim had received a new set of orders, assigning him to be the Executive Assistant to the Assistant Secretary of the Navy. The importance of the job depends on how many 'Assistants' there are in the title. His boss was a retired Brigadier General of the Marine Corps and being single, he preferred gorgeous blonde starlets. On the night of the Ball, the General appeared at the entrance with one of these. She was wrapped in a full -length chinchilla coat. I had never seen a full - length chinchilla coat except on Joan Crawford on the big screen. Because Gorgeous preferred not to check it, she swept into the huge room in all her furry glory and was guided to our table.

As she approached, Jim said under his breath, "You're in charge of the coat."

"You've got to be kidding. Do I wear it, kill it or steal it?" He was not amused. Neither was I.

But, to hear is to obey.

Navy Balls are not my favorite form of entertainment. Dancing around the floor, the men stop and tell each other sea stories. The wives swap information on each other's children and in that day and age, nobody was too anxious to elaborate on what their children were up to.

Wedged into shoes that hurt, with a back tired from walking the halls of Congress, I faced the prospect of 'taking charge of the coat'. Resigned, I returned to the table, took up my mission, slipped off my shoes and stared at several hundred pelts of several hundred unfortunate chinchillas.

After ten long minutes alone and with no one to talk to, I laid a silky fur coat sleeve on the table and put Gorgeous's jeweled purse at the end of it. Hoping it looked like there was a body inside the mass of luxury, I marched to the ladies' lounge and sulked for nearly an hour. Call it a rebellion, I had simply had it with orders from headquarters.

Unfortunately, nobody missed me for that hour and when I returned to the table, several hundred chinchillas were waiting for my undivided attention while Gorgeous was dancing with every eligible and some not so eligible officers there.

But the General knew how to throw a good party of his own. The Decatur House is just one block from the White House across from Lafayette Square. Its charm lay in its age and design and for special people, it was available for entertaining. The General fit the category and one evening, we were summoned to a formal dinner party. Jim would escort the General's mother, a delightfully candid woman in her eighties, who had edgy, but loving words about her son. My partner for the evening was Raymond Burr of *Perry Mason* fame. Among the guests were Senator John Warner and Robert Strauss, advisor to the President. We mingled, ate caviar, held in our stomachs and felt rather posh.

Resplendent in a perfectly tailored tuxedo, cuffs and jabot of Belgian lace, Mr. Burr, who became Raymond five minutes into the first course, held me spellbound with his description of his privately owned South Pacific island, studded with Charolais cattle, palm trees and natives he adopted as his own. Later, I would learn of the high school girls and boys he brought to the United States in order to provide them with college educations.

My evening was stellar. There were no small dead rodents to watch.

The following year, the Brigadier General went on to marry a beautiful New York model with the wedding reception at the Quantico Marine Base in Virginia.

During the festivities, which included a very large and intricately carved ice sculpture, I was given the assignment of clearing the Club of all guests. Reports of a bomb placed in the building made it mandatory we all move to the lawn outside. The temperature was near the ninety-eight degree mark with matching humidity. The guests and the ice sculpture melted at approximately the same rate.

Despite the drama, no bomb was found and after an hour, we trooped back into the reception room to a puddle where the ice sculpture had been.

Jim was working in the Pentagon fourteen to sixteen hours a day and Jeff waited at the front door to shake his hand before going to bed. I lost count of the number of meals that went into the garbage disposal. Typical Washington duty.

As I was getting ready to leave for work one morning, he called from his office.

"Thought I should alert you. There are peaceniks lying down all over the roadway of the Fourteenth Street Bridge. They're protesting the war, of course."

"Would you rather I didn't go into the office?" How sweet of him to be concerned about my safety.

"No, it's okay to go to work, just don't run over any of them."

Later, these same protestors marched on Capitol Hill and the great Longworth Building doors were shut. Watching from other offices that fronted on the scene, we saw a skinny, grubby longhaired naked man stumble up the Capitol steps. He only managed to look pathetic. This same mob had quartered on the Mall during their week of protests and left it ruined.

On my way home from the office that day, Marines in combat dress, with fixed bayonets, lined the Fourteenth Street Bridge. When I made it across, I pulled off the road onto the shoulder shaking with anger that my country was under siege by these grimy malcontents.

On July sixteenth 1969, men walked on the moon for the first time. The moment was electric and for once, the American public celebrated accomplishment. Out for an evening walk, we studied the moon and wondered if Neil Armstrong, on a stroll around the block, ever looked at it and said, *My footprints are up there.* What a contrast to the unruly mob on the mall that only managed to make love, smoke pot and wave signs, damning their country.

In May of '71, a bomb was found in one of the Senate bathrooms.

CHAPTER TWENTY ONE

December 1971 Garmish, Bavaria

We tumbled out of the taxi, stiff from the long train ride from Frankfurt, Germany to Garmisch, Bavaria. Jeff was in charge of the skis, Jim hauled the luggage out of the trunk and I stood transfixed by the inky sky, shot with brilliant bits of light.

"What beautiful stars. I've never seen them so bright."

The cabdriver chuckled, speaking in broken English. "Those aren't stars, they're hotels."

My God, that's where we would be skiing and it was straight up. My bunny slope expertise began to look somewhat inadequate.

Jeff had taken up skiing, was a natural, and the only way we would ever see him face to face, was to join him. I was not a natural. Every time I faced the bunny slopes in Pennsylvania, there was the dry taste of terror in my mouth. But investing in skis, bindings, poles, boots and the mountain of clothing that goes along with it, prompted us to leave Washington for the Christmas holidays and fly to Germany to try the slopes with the big guys. Jeff and his father were still getting reacquainted and this trip looked like a good way for the two of them to be together without the eternal interference from the Pentagon.

"Where the hell is the snow? We come all this way and there's no snow." Jim was logically annoyed because Europe was cold and bare. It had been a dry winter and we all felt ridiculous, carrying our equipment like the tourists we were.

"They said there was snow in Garmish. Something abut a glacier." I could see an argument shaping up. "Do we have to carry all this stuff up to a glacier?"

"No, dear. First, you put it on your body and then carry it up to the glacier."

Jeff grinned. "Dad, if there's a glacier, there's snow and glaciers don't go away overrnight." More logic. Jim subsided.

Leaving Frankfurt on the train, we looked back as we left the train station. The building was cratered with bomb and bullet holes, remnants of the Allied bombings of this vital railway hub. The Germans, usually such particular people had chosen to leave the destruction as a statement. Twenty-five years had done little to soften its appearance.

The German people on the train held unending conversations with each other and at dusk, we neared a stop. Suddenly, the talk ceased. Eyes looked down. There was nothing but the rhythmic clatter of wheels on rails.

Jeff asked, "What is it, Mom?"

I was as puzzled as he was at the silence in the car. Looking out the window, the countryside had gone from pleasant to bleak. The landscape looked blasted. Nothing grew and nothing moved. As we rolled into the station, I saw the name of the town on the side of the depot.

Dachau.

"We'll talk later, Jeff. Now is not a good time."

The silence lasted until well past the area, then conversation began again and I softly filled Jeff in on the meaning of the town.

The ski slope was straight up, somewhere in the vicinity of Valhalla. We boarded a train before dawn and began the ascent to the glacier. I had the distinct feeling I was riding to my death.

On the train was a company of German soldiers with skis, poles and determined chins. When the train stopped at the top of the mountain, instead of transferring the men to the cable car to cross the glacier and ski down to the lift line, the door opened and the soldiers marched stoically to an eighteen-inch wide path of solid ice that went straight down. They strapped on their skis and one by one, getting a push from their instructor, skied for the first time down the suicidal slope. If they weren't terrified, I was.

Months before, on short, wooden skis that liked me, I had learned the art of getting to the bottom of something at uncontrollable speed with solid objects to be avoided. My first time on a PemnsylvaniaT Bar found me falling off headfirst into a snow bank. Picked up by the waistband on my jeans, shaken like a snow-covered puppy, set upright and given a not-too-gentle push to start me on the way down the slope, I careened past startled skiers until I ran into a solid object that stopped me. Luckily, it was not Jim who did this dastardly deed, but a friend of his whose tall and elegant wife looked like she had been born on skis and had just won an Olympics gold.

In the lift line on the Zugspitze glacier, a forest of ski poles, held by determined, serious-faced people of all ages, moved slowly forward toward the T bars that would carry them to the top of the glacier that looked like Everest from the bottom. Among the poles were two that were moving backward. They were mine. Jim and Jeff were ahead of me and I hoped they wouldn't notice this gray-faced coward who eventually sat in a snowdrift and tried not to look terrified.

A compact medium-sized man of undetermined age because of his tanned leathery face, helped me to my feet, and introduced himself as 'Gus'. In broken English, he told me he had been a mountain climber, ski instructor and guide for sixty years and would like to help me get to the top. Gratefully, since nobody else was offering anything constructive and I was having a lousy time, I accepted. We somehow managed to sit on the T-bar. Staring down at my feet buckled into the new skis Jim had proudly given me for our trip, and wishing they were short and wooden, I concentrated on keeping them in the icy ruts carved in the snow. The skis stretched out in front of me like railroad tracks.

Gus said, "Look up. Look up. You Americans always look down. See the beauty out here before you." I was going to the top with a poet. for heaven's sake.

"Gus, if I look up, I'll flip off this flipping T-bar."

He put his head back and laughed, looking all the time like the T-bar was a part of his anatomy. At the top of the glacier, three sets of Alps stretched out and all around us. I would have been content to simply stare at this magnificent sight for the rest of the day, but no such luck, down it was. Patiently, Gus guided me from one side of the glacier to the other. Halfway down, we stopped to rest. Suddenly, a body flashed by between us and we both looked after it.

"Olympics", said Gus, admiringly.

"My son", said I, proudly. We both grinned. Jeff was so at home and loose on skis, he reminded me of Ichabod Crane.

The next day found me in the village, shopping and sipping hot chocolate. The boys were on the mountain again and I could see clouds of snow over the glacier. Jim came back to the hotel about three without Jeff. and casually said our son wanted to stay until it was too dark to ski. My motherly instincts kicked into high gear.

"Jim, my God, it's a blizzard up there. You left your youngest child on a 14,000 foot mountain all by himself? How could you do that?'

"He's not alone and he's having a great time. He would have been unhappy if I dragged him back here because I was cold." He didn't seem too concerned and I paced the floor until Jeff strolled in, tired, grinning and soaked to the skin.

They skied for the next six days as I pursued my comparisons of hot chocolate in the quaint little town. Th en, bundling up the mountain of equipment, we trudged to the train station to begin the trip back to Washington, D.C.

Jim continued to receive medals for his efforts during the last cruise. A friend of mine took one look at him in full dress uniform and said, "Tilt". We teased him about it, but knowing what went into the earning of those awards, it was a gentle tease.

The previous year, Jamey, her husband Bob and their new baby, Anna, had come home for Christmas. Any estrangement was gone. We had a Charles Dickens' Christmas with only the goose missing, and our family was solid once again. The baby, Anna was the binding force that brought us together and I marveled that we resumed our loving relationship with such ease.

May 1971

After three years in Washington, new orders were cut. Jim received his first ship command. This meant that he had 'screened' for an aircraft carrier. The Navy's rule was a man should have command of a 'deep draft' ship before he can take a carrier. As an aviator, he had to learn the basics from the bilges to the bridge. 'Blackshoes' (surface Navy men) took a dim view of aviators driving a ship. The pressures were obvious and Jim could hardly wait.

Jeff graduated from the High School he had attended for a full three years. His father assumed he would go to the Naval Academy and all the necessary arrangements had been made.

One spring evening, he asked to speak to us both. I had an uneasy feeling about our coming conversation, and only hoped there would be no bombs dropped.

"Dad, a long time ago, you told me that when the time came to choose what I want to do for the rest of my life, the decision would be mine." He looked serious and hopeful. I resisted the urge to smooth back the blonde lock of hair on his forehead. "I don't want a naval career. I want to go to college, study what I choose to and figure out what to do with my life. I don't want the Navy doing it for me."

There was a long silence while we let this sink in. Instinctively, I knew Jeff had had enough of military life and would go into it only under duress. There was shock and disappointment on Jim's face, but proudly, I watched him keep his anger in control.

. It's hard, telling a man who has risked his life for his country so many times that his son wants to take another direction. Having a hero for a father can carry its own set of problems, not the least of which is, 'How does one ever live up to that?' I chose not to tell Jim of all the difficulties our children had faced because of our way of life. He was my husband. I would not diminish his successes.

Eventually and with our blessing, Jeffrey chose the University of Iowa, our home state and we prepared for another move, this time, back to Norfolk and our White House.

Patricia Linder

CHAPTER TWENTY TWO

June 1971 found Jim as the new Commanding Officer of the USS Sylvania. After six years and three moves, we were once again in Virginia Beach. The territory was familiar to me and for the first time in twenty-three years, we moved back into the same house.

This was a new world for both of us. The Sylvania was a support ship, supplying everything from ice cream and lettuce to nuts and bolts. Underway replenishments means sidling up to another ship at sea and transferring whatever they needed. In brisk seas, the possibility of collision was always there and as every Navy man knows, a collision at sea can ruin your whole day. A 'paper collision' means that the distance between the ship being replenished and the replenishing ship is only the thickness of a piece of paper. By careful sleuthing, I unearthed this piece of information and wished I hadn't.

Sylvania came out of the shipyard in 1964, cost 22.5 million dollars with a birth weight of 17,500 tons and was 581 feet long. As the crew was fond of saying, "It must have been a beautiful baby, 'cause baby, look at her now," which brings up the question, why are ships referred to as female?

Jim explained that in the old days, ships sported well-endowed female figureheads. He could only guess that if the 'old girl' couldn't go aboard and sail with her husband, they put a wooden 'old girl' on the front, instead. My own assessment was – a sailor is a sailor the world around, and that wooden 'old girl' may have been the only one they saw at sea for months or years at a time.

She was Navy gray, nothing unusual in that, but she looked very big to me. Of course I had spent time on aircraft carriers, the biggest of all Navy ships, but my husband was responsible for this one, and it made a difference.

The Change of Command was held aboard the ship in its berth at the Norfolk Naval Station and the uniform of the day was 'dress whites'. Seeing an entire ship's complement in white uniforms is a memorable sight. Their posture is straighter, their demeanor more serious.

Following the ceremony on the helicopter deck, we climbed down the ladder to Jim's stateroom, followed by our family and guests. Jim spoke to each one, then disappeared into his bedroom to change out of his dress uniform.. His Executive Officer tapped on the door, entering hurriedly.

"Mrs. Linder, we have an emergency aboard and I need to speak to the Captain."

Hurriedly, I slipped into Jim's bedroom and said, "Your XO is in the other room and there is an emergency. Do you want him to come in here or wait until you're dressed"

"In here, a.s.a.p."

In the middle of putting on his pants, Jim was informed that the 'Flag Bag' was on fire. His command was less than thirty minutes old. Any kind of fire on a ship has the potential of a major catastrophe and an even bigger one with dignitaries and guests aboard.

The Flag Bag is just that – a bag where they store the signal flags. Being cloth, they would easily burn. How or why it started was anybody's guess, but the speed with which Jim moved ensured the emergency would be swiftly dealt with. With hardly a ripple, the matter was resolved and he rejoined his guests.

When Jim took the ship in June, the schedule read 'Deploy to the Mediterranean in February'. Because every hour of every day was a learning one, I saw little of him. In August, an all-hands party was arranged and we attended as 'the new Skipper and his wife'. It was quite a night.

As we entered the large room, the first thing I saw was one long table with nothing but officers and their wives. Scattered around the room were smaller tables with 'the crew'. One section of the room near the back wall, held only black enlisted personnel, as was the custom. Being new at this ship's company game, I wondered how the evening would evolve.

We were placed dead center at the long table facing a room full of strangers. Nothing new, here. This had happened with every duty change. But there was tension in the air. Jim was an aviator and the rest of the officers were 'blackshoes' (surface Navy). I could feel the reservations they had. Their wives looked me over, wary and critical. Conversation was brief and cool; the usual questions about children – safe topic – they knew we had some. Nothing about where we came from or what our previous lives had been like. I felt we had no past. We began with this evening.

But there was another tension. This was the era of racial problems in the Navy. Tradition had automatically imposed segregation and now, the feeling was one of change. After dinner was served, a band began to play dance music. A tall, rangy black sailor detached himself from his table in the back of the room, walked its length and positioned himself directly in front of me.

His face was expressionless when he looked down and asked, "Will you dance with me?"

Out of the corner of my eye, I saw several officers push their chairs back and rise to their feet, obviously anticipating trouble.

Without turning to Jim, I looked at the man, pushed my own chair back and said, "Thank you. I would like that."

With every eye watching me, I walked the length of the table, rounded the corner, and onto the center of the dance floor. The music was *Joy in the Morning*. I realized this was no fox trot. Looking up at him, I grinned, looked down at his fee and asked, "What do I do now?"

He said, "You move."

I did.

Not a soul joined us for that dance. Here I was, the Skipper's wife, alone with a black man on the dance floor trying to figure out how to do the same thing he was doing.

He grinned. "You must have teenagers. You're pretty good."

I relaxed and realized we were actually having fun.

I knew we had made points – he with his people and I with mine. The music changed and Jim asked the Executive Officer's wife to dance. Thee tall young sailor escorted me back to my chair, thanked me and glided back to his table of friends with a grin on his face. If a bet had been made, he won it. And won it like a gentleman.

I was met by shocked and dubious looks at the long table which came as no surprise. Ignoring them, I said yes to the Executive Officer when he dutifully asked me to join the other dancers.

Normally, the Commanding Officer and his wife are the first to leave any party. That night, we were the last. It was fun once everyone relaxed. Eventually, the thaw became complete and as we said goodnight, the tall, rangy black sailor saluted me. From that night on, it was a great tour of duty. Jim's ship problems were only the usual ones and the wives recognized me as an individual in my own right, not just the Skipper's wife.

We had Christmas together that year, with Jeff home from college for the holidays. He was doing well. His name was on the Dean's list and he looked relaxed and contented.

The ship left for the Med in February and my suitcase was packed in March, after school spring vacation came to an end. This time it was Spain. The ship would put into Malaga on the Costa del Sol, Spain's Riviera and I was there to meet it. The other wives were amazed that a wife would do such a thing. By the time I left, three others had decided to go along with me. By tradition, surface Navy wives usually remained at home, but obviously not as their choice. Aviators' wives are a different breed. Living in perpetual fear for our husband's lives gives us the courage to be where he is. Like the flu, it was catching. I'm sure their husbands would happily have throttled me because of the expense, but memories were made that would last them a lifetime.

Spain was a new country with new challenges. As always, I was living on my allotment money and had to make it stretch. Introducing the other wives to 'the menu of the day', -- every country has one -- they learned to sleep late, eat one big meal at noon, then tapas for dinner. Tapas are the Spanish hors d'oeuvre and for little money, they will carry you through until the next day's lunch.

We made it in time to stand on Fleet Landing and watch our husbands' ship, the Sylvania nose into port, American flag flying. As I spent the next few years, marching around the Mediterranean in pursuit of my husband, I came to realize what the sight of that flag meant.

To the wives it looked like home that day and as the men left the ship to explore Malaga's Spanish delights, it remained flying as a symbol of safe haven. To the Spanish business- man, it meant money. To Spain, it meant NATO and protection.

Jim was loath to leave the ship for any reason. He was not just enjoying every minute of his command, he felt the heavy weight of responsibility. But I was there and being as patient as possible, I coaxed him off for a day in Torremelinos, a resort town a few miles up the coast from Malaga. Not knowing it was the favorite watering hole for Swedish blonde goddess secretaries on vacation during the winter months, I anticipated a leisurely, romantic day in the sun, sipping sangria over a plate of paella with the sparkling

Mediterranean at our feet. Instead, I got sporadic conversation that dwindled off as Jim spotted one of his sailors on a forbidden motorcycle with a goddess clothed in little more than her wallet.

But we managed a picnic in Granada, a stroll through the Alhambra and danced a bolero without castanets in a dim Spanish bodega. Jim's Executive Officer learned how to be a Commanding Officer while Jim took a few well-earned hours off. It worked out. He left, I packed and headed north to Barcelona, his next port of call.

. In the Catalan city of Barcelona, we strolled on a Sunday, through one of the many green parks near the Templo Expiatorio Sagrada Familia. the cathedral of the Sagrada family.

In the park, couples walked slowly, forming a large circle. The ladies put their purses into the center, then joining hands, the men and women began a slow, stately slide of a dance. Hands reached out to clasp ours, my purse joined the others and we were drawn into the circle. The steps were simple, but the pace never varied, a piper played a song and we swayed and moved to his rhythm. The dance was the soldana, the moment, pure magic.

In the years to come, I would be in Barcelona many times, enjoying the bookstalls and birds in cages on the Ramblas, exploring the oldest part of the city, the Gut and learning the people. My fascination with Baracelona never dimmed. Even sleeping in a hostel on a bedbug ridden straw mattress because of an international soccer game, failed to lessen my affection for her. She epitomized the Catalan, haughty with Spanish pride.

The ship left and my money ran out. Reluctantly, I flew home, but with the knowledge there would be another cruise. I would see Spain again.

CHAPTER TWENTY THREE

Home looked good. The glories of Spain in the 70's included pensions with grimy walls, rancid butter and bad plumbing. 'Europe on five dollars a day' never was a truth and often, I yearned for our rambling, White House with its dogwoods and azalea bushes. The quaintness of ancient plumbing will never compare to a good toilet that flushes.

Jeff threw us a curve. Despite making the Dean's list both semesters, he decided to transfer to the University of Texas to continue his college education. Austin had good music and he felt, more to offer. To protect us from a whopping tuition bill, he established himself, found a job, worked a year and became a resident. All of this was begun while I was following his father around the Mediterranean. Life goes on. As much as I wanted to box his ears for putting us through another uncertain time, we had made a promise. It wasn't easy for him. Jobs in college towns are notoriously low in pay and he learned just how little he could do with a dollar., a lesson that would stay with him. He was on his own and liked the independence of making decisions. I had learned that I would always have to make a choice between my children and my husband. It could not be both.

Jim turned over the Sylvania to its new Commanding Officer and prepared to take command of the aircraft carrier USS Forrestal– CVA – 59, the ship that had nearly been destroyed by fire during the Vietnam war. His promotions had come steadily as the jobs he was assigned required particular ranks and he more than met the qualifications. Making Captain while in Washington, D.C., moved him into the heady atmosphere of ship commands and during the Sylvania's cruise back to the United States, he received his next set of orders. We would always have a special feeling for the Sylvani and left its good people with regret.

October, 1972

For the next three months, Jim was trained in the art of handling an aircraft carrier and its full complement of five thousand people when on cruise. . The magnitude of it left me breathless. Because my husband was responsible for it, the ship looked larger than any other carrier to me.

Jim flew to Athens, Greece for the Change of Command in October and I followed in November. The cruise would be ten months long due to the possibility of home porting the ship in Greece. Negotiations were afoot, but it was still a question of feasibility. My big yellow suitcase was packed to the hilt with three season's clothes and so heavy, my legs crossed when I tried to carry it.

For the first time in my European travels, I felt completely at home when I walked into Athens' International airport. Even with no knowledge of the language, I had no problem finding the couple waiting to meet me. They were Jim's friends and Captain Fields was on the Admiral's staff that was attached to Jim's ship. We hurriedly left for their apartment, where I was instructed to eat my dinner and go to bed. Jim had asked that they take me to the ship at midnight to board for a dependents' cruise. Minding well, I obeyed. Promptly at midnight, we were in their car with the big yellow suitcase in the trunk, on our way to Fleet Landing.

It was a madhouse. Over one hundred wives and children were being loaded aboard this giant of a ship with luggage, umbrellas, teddy bears and anything else they would need for the next few days. My big yellow bag joined the others and some poor sailor had the unenviable job of hauling it down to Jim's stateroom.

Our destination was the island of Rhodes, a day's sail from Athens. The previous CO had laid on the dependents' cruise and Jim inherited it when he took the ship. It was not something a new Commanding Officer would prefer to do upon taking a carrier for the first time. Wives and kiddies can be a problem on dry land. At sea, they were a potential disaster. The Admiral, his family and his Staff came aboard. An officer stashed me in Jim's stateroom, passing along the word the Captain would join me after the ship got under way. We had yet to see each other. When we did, Jim looked harried and distracted. There had been little time for sleep for either of us and I saw shadows under his eyes. I thought of the long day ahead.

It was nearly morning when the ship left for Rhodes. Jim took me to the bridge with him where he stayed for the duration of the trip to Rhodes. After we left the harbor, we steamed due south and as the sky lightened, I noticed two other ships, one on either side of us, looking very much like a convoy. The navigator explained they were Russian ships that had been tailing the Forrestal during its sea time and on into the Athens harbor. Apparently the two ships assumed the

Forrestal would remain in port and they shut down their boilers. But the carrier, with wives and children safely aboard, sailed majestically past the two unfriendlies and headed to sea. The two Russsian captains, much to their chagrin, must have scrambled to get up steam to follow. I doubted they were pleased with the situation. One never did get the boilers properly working and limped along, blowing black smoke. Jim sent a message, offering assistance but was met with a stony silence.

To give the dependents an idea of what their husbands did for a living, flight operations were ordered. Planes launched by catapult and landed on the flight deck, catching wires to stop them. The sound of the screaming cables as they were released for the next plane only added to the excitement. Men performed their jobs with precision and the seriousness of a ship at war. What looked like frantic scrambling on the flight deck was instead, a choreographed dance of danger and the expertise to live through each launch and recovery. The adrenaline was pumping on the bridge as I sat quietly in a corner out of the way.

The day was perfect until we neared Rhodes. A mistral storm out of North Africa slammed the ship with high winds and all was secured. The seas and the big carrier began to roll. Jim's face was grim and tight with worry. By Navy law, the dependents had to be off the ship at sundown. Launching small boats in high seas was a dicey thing at best and today, there was no best. In trying to set the two sixty thousand pound anchors on the rock bottom, it became apparent they would not catch. A certain amount of jockeying back and forth had to be done and with a ship the size of the Forrestal, it was done very carefully. The Admiral called the bridge from his quarters asking what was going on. A hatch slammed on his teenage daughter's hand and an emergency was declared for the flight surgeon.

A young sailor tried to enter the bridge area, but the armed Marine on guard kept him behind his outstretched arm. The man wanted to see the Skipper.

Darkness had fallen early. The bridge was lighted by red running lights and the atmosphere was deadly calm and tense in the eerie glow. Finally, with the anchor set, Jim nodded to the stoic Marine who let the young sailor onto the bridge.

At attention, he walked to the Captain's chair, saluted and said, "Skipper, I want to report there are weevils in the flour."

It was so ludicrous, I had to clamp my jaws shut to keep from laughing. Jim stared at the boy for a moment, then picked up his phone and very quietly said, "Get me the Supply Officer – *now*."

The wives and children made ready to board the small boats tossing on the boiling sea. It was announced their husbands could not leave the ship to accompany them. Another American ship – a destroyer – had lost its anchor and was drifting toward the Forrestal. Because of the danger to the dependents, Jim , feeling as responsible for their safety of the men's families as he did for his ship, chose to accompany us into Fleet Landing. Once on Rhodes, the wives and children scattered to find their hotels and Jim made ready to return to the ship, but the mistral had strengthened and the boats could not leave the pier. H was stuck on land with the possibility of another ship colliding with his. By walkie talkie, the Executive Officer informed him that a sailor had just jumped overboard.

I felt in the way.

I must say, Jim was unflappable. Only the jumping muscles in his jaw belied his outward calm.

He paced the hotel room during the uneasy night. It was another night without sleep. The next day, the mistral ended, the men came ashore to find their wives and explore the island for the few days we would be there. Jim returned to his ship, relieved the disaster of a collision had been averted. The lost sailor whose body washed ashore weeks later, had jumped overboard after reading a letter from his sweetheart, saying she had married another man.

Jim had stories to tell me about the first few weeks of his new command. Still in the States, waiting for the time we had arranged to meet in Athens., I missed his first cruise to Thessaloniki, a port city on the Ageean Sea, north of Athens.

"There I was with a new command, a ship and crew I knew nothing about and we're coming into the Thess harbor. The fog was so bad, I could hardly see past the bridge."

"I thought you had to anchor out in weather like that."

He sighed. "We had the Admiral aboard. He reminded me of the diplomats, waiting to meet with him and besides, his wife and kids were waiting in Thess, and his word was, 'You're the Captain and the decision is yours', but I knew it was important for him to make his meetings, so we kept steaming. I didn't know if my navigator knew there were rocks around, but in we went. Then we began to hear some really weird noises off both the port and starboard sides. The fishing boats had been caught in the same fog we were and they were making noises to keep us from hitting them. One guy was beating on a dishpan! This was a 70,000 ton ship and this guy in a rowboat is beating on a dishpan to make us stop."

"One of the officers said, 'Sir, there's a boatload of women up against the ship.' It turned out the wives of the men on the ship had come to Thessaloniki, rented a boat and were out there to come aboard. We hadn't even anchored. We were still underway."

I knew policy would be changed on that one.

Returning to Athens from Rhodes, the Forrestal deposited wives, children, luggage and me on the dock and steamed back to sea. So much for lingering goodbyes. Jim had had enough of wives and kiddies to last him a lifetime.

One of my new friends invited me to share her apartment until I could find one of my own. We zipped around Athens in her little MG, checking out contacts and finally found a place in a small village called Glyfada, the resort for the Athenians who came to the Aegean Sea for the summer. My apartment was tiny but attractive with only a walk out the door to be on the beach. It belonged to an airline pilot and was directly in the flight path for incoming planes.

One early morning, strolling along the water's edge, I noticed a gray-haired man in a long, black overcoat walking ahead of me. In his hands clasped behind him, he held silver worry beads. His head was bowed and his shoulders shook. When he reversed direction, I was startled to find myself facing Aristotle Onassis. His son

Alexander had just been killed at the controls of his own plane as he came in for a landing. Mr.Onassis was staying at his sister's house, next door to my apartment building. Hiding in his grief, her home provided the only place he could get away from the press.

My building's supervisor George treated me as an accident waiting to happen. It was sleeting and very cold the night I moved into my apartment. Climbing the marble stairs to the second floor, I unlocked the door, turned on the lights and plugging in the five radiators, promptly blew out the electricity in the whole building. With no lights and only a vague recollection of the floor plan, I closed the door and dropped to the marble floor. On hands and knees, dragging the big yellow suitcase behind me, I felt the way into what my memory said was the bedroom. Trying to unlock the suitcase in pitch darkness was impossible. With no lights or heat, I climbed into bed with my clothes on and huddled under a thin blanket for the rest of the night.

Morning found short, stocky George eye to eye with me at my door, ready to evict this crazy woman for blowing out the electricity. But one look at my frozen, weary form changed his mind and with hand gestures and a gabble of words, he managed to make me understand what I should not do again. He seemed satisfied with my promise to behave.

George became my friend, calling me "The Captain's woman" because of Jim's brief and sporadic visits. I never knew if he thought we were married or unmarried, but the first time Jim appeared in full uniform, George was visibly impressed and periodically, presented me with gifts from the sea. As well as being the building supervisor, he was a fisherman and proudest when he held a dead squid as an offering for my next meal. Not having the faintest idea what to do with a dead squid, the dangling creature was often stuffed into my tote bag and on those early morning walks, returned to the sea.

The ship made port again in Thessaloniki and this time, I flew in to meet it. In the interim, the wives and I organized into a cohesive group. One hundred twenty-one women and children either moved as a pack, or separately, depending on health problems, finances or side trip arrangements. We were all living on our monthly allotments, although some of the women had to depend only on what their husbands handed them in the way of money before they left on the ship. Many remained in Athens because there was not enough cash for an airline ticket.

In Thess this time, no wives bumped up against the ship. Word was sent out to them to remain on shore until the liberty boats tied up and then, and only then would they be allowed to go out to the ship. That order had Jim's fingerprint all over it.

In the seventies, short island tours were available that fit our budget and as often as we had the funds, the wives hopped a boat and explored the Greek Islands. Women traveling alone were an oddity. On a one- day trip to Hydra, a tiny, picturesque piece of real estate, I stood at the railing of the ship to watch the currents and the birds. At certain times of the day, the Aegean Sea explodes with light like no other body of water in the world. A possible explanation is the vast number of islands and the many currents that swirl around them.

The Captain of the ship appeared at my elbow and introduced himself. He seemed worried about something and in halting English, asked me if I was all right. I assured him I was enjoying watching the light on the water and its complicated currents.

"But you are alone and you were looking into the water." He appeared to be genuinely worried. I guessed he thought I was contemplating ending it all with a jump into the Aegean Sea.

"I'm fine. Please don't be concerned. The birds are waiting to be fed and there is leftover bread from my sandwich. I'm alone because my husband is on another ship and can't be with me."

That sharpened his interest and brought on a further question. "Why is he on another ship?"

I studied this ordinary Greek man who looked like he belonged on a fishing boat instead of one full of tourists. His Captain's uniform was worn but spotless; his features, classic. Making the daily run to Hydra and back was undoubtedly a bore, yet the sea is so much a part of the people of Greece, I knew he was in his proper element.

"My husband is aboard the American aircraft carrier that comes into Athens."

He looked me over carefully, then asked, "Is he an officer?"

"Yes, he is."

Tilting his head to one side, he said, "I guessed right, okay?"

"You did."

"What does he do for his job on that big ship?

"He mostly tells other people what to do."

A triumphant smile lighted his face. "Ah, he is the Captain. Like me."

I smiled. "Like you."

He bowed slightly, then invited me to see his bridge and meet the crew, and when I accepted, he led the way to a square room above the passenger deck.

"You shall have a cup of our fine Greek coffee."

His manner was courtly and respectful. Proudly, he introduced his crew. I nodded and murmured a few appropriate Greek words of greeting as we shook hands.

A table the size of a chess board was placed, two straight-backed chairs, a snowy cloth with two napkins and in miniature cups, black Greek coffee, one half of which is sludge. No sugar was offered and I did not request it.

As we sipped, he asked me questions about America. Many Greek people` I met had at least one relative somewhere in the United States and it was always with great pride, they named the city. He asked about the Forrestal and my answers were general and guarded.

At last, he told me what was wrong with my country.

His dark brows formed a straight line above the serious expression in his eyes. "When your country helps another, your country always wants to be thanked." For a moment, he was embarrassed by his own words, then looking directly at me he waited for my response.

"And is that wrong?" I was not angry, merely curious at his choice of words.

He spoke firmly but with kindness. "You should give the money ......then go without waiting for a thank you." .

"Is that the way of your country?" I was genuinely intrigued.

"It's the way we keep our....." He searched for the word...."pride."

I gave this some thought and after a few moments, said, "Thank you for teaching me a very important thing. My husband will be interested in what you have said."

He beamed.

The rest of the day, I was treated like visiting royalty, helped back aboard the ship at sailing time in Hydra and served another cup of coffee on the small bridge. He secured a taxi for me when we landed and we shook hands, bowed formally to each other and I thanked him for his honesty. It occurred to me that he should meet Jim sometime.

The Greek people became my friends. The flower lady in Glyfada always tucked a blossom over my ear when I stopped to say hello and the skirted policeman in the middle of the street, directed traffic to stop, then motioned me to cross with a kindly "Kalimera" (good morning). They were intense people, hard like their land, but with the joy of knowing that their country was 'the cradle of civilization' and their culture had survived for centuries.

At the end of the Second World War, after a long and difficult German occupation, communism moved into the vacuum the enemy left. With most of its population weak from starvation, the Greeks beat back a communist takeover. But as they left the country, the Russians swept it clean of the children of Greece. They kidnapped as many as they could, took them back to Russia, 're-educated' them, then returned them as young adults to infiltrate their own country with the communist doctrine. If they could not take it by force, they would take it from within. They were unsuccessful. As much as the Greeks loved their children, they shunned them when they returned. It was a country of heartbreak.

July 1974

Rounding the corner of the Grand Bretagne Hotel in Syntagma Square, I came face to face with a tank cannon. Earlier that morning, I heard a brief report on the Stars and Stripes radio station about unrest in Athens. The 'unrest' was a military coup and my errand put me in the middle of it. On the way to the market to buy apples, it was clear that another route was advisable. Skirting the obvious signs of a military action, I shakily found the apple stall, made my purchase, forgoing my usual treat of a spinach cheese pie and hurried to the bus to Glyfada. President Papadopoulus was being overthrown by the military under the direction of Lt.General Kazikis who eventually moved into the presidency. Having learned something about the complexities of Greek politics, I would stay out of town for a while.

Patricia Linder

CHAPTER TWENTY FOUR

Athens, 1973

Watergate blossomed in Washington, D.C. in all of its dubious glory. Having worked on Capitol Hill, names were familiar and I felt sadness at the impression we were giving the rest of the world. Congressman Zion had occasionally complained how isolated President Nixon was from the realities of political life. His staff kept him unavailable, even to the members of his own Party. It was frustrating to be a Republican in the 70's. The White House was a bastion of power, guarded from all by the fierce loyalty of the President's Staff. Many who came into public service with Nixon, went out with him.

The Armed Forces radio station carried the hearings. To many Europeans, it was a tempest in a teacup, compared to the political aberrations that abounded in nearly every other country. But despite the shabbiness of it all, the importance of the law of our land was crystal clear. Justice counted and that raised our esteem in the eyes of the world. Corruption was not taken for granted and if it brought down a president, so be it. The U.S. was firmly established as a country that lives by its laws.

In the ten months the Forrestal stayed in the Mediterranean, the schedule was a busy one. War games with other NATO countries took the ship into other foreign waters. Because of the oil shortage in the United States, ship speeds were reduced, time at sea and in the air pared down. In order to keep the Air Wing combat ready, Jim took

217

the carrier to the bottom of Greece's Peloponnesus Peninsula where the mountain ranges provided winds strong enough to launch planes from a stationary flight deck. Positioning the Forrestal into the winds, a new term was developed – flankering – or flying planes with the ship at anchor. It was one way to conserve oil.

Each time the ship left for an at-sea period, and if there was a port call other than Athens, suitcases were packed, reservations made and the wives left for Mallorca, Spain, Italy or Corfu.

The ship 'cross-decked' with the British aircraft carrier, Ark Royal in Rota, Spain. For three days, the two ships exchanged men, planes and ideas.

The Pretender to the throne of Spain – the Infante – invited us to lunch. He was in his eighties, flew his own plane, owned a parrot and perched on his shoulder, the parrot owned him, telling him when to take his nap and when to go to bed. He lived in a sprawling, Spanish hacienda, north of Rota. Tall and slender, this Spanish don was a true aristocrat. A high forehead was fringed by a halo of white hair and his dark eyes sparkled with interest above a classic Spanish nose. His stance was that of a matador executing a manoletina pass. This was no Pretender to the throne, the Infante belonged on it.

From early childhood, he kept a daily diary. With pride, he unlocked steel doors to show me the volumes of history recorded in his own hand. The story of Spain for the preceding eighty years lived in those books. With the Franco government one of dictatorship, and the Spanish Civil War of the thirties, they were explosive.

He had met and talked with Ernest Hemingway and of course, wrote of his visit. Smiling, he told me our afternoon with him would be recorded before he slept for the night. I was completely charmed by his old -world gallantry.

In March 1973, torrential rains flooded the country of Tunisia, North Africa and the Forrestal steamed to its shores to aid in the rescue and evacuation of people and animals. Helicopters lifted the stranded, frantic Tunisians to dry land where food and clothing could be provided. For ten days, the carrier participated in the rescue. In addition to the 19,000 meals routinely served to the men on the ship twenty-four hours of every day, the galley turned out great quantities of food that were airlifted by the same helos that would evacuate the people. At the end of the operation, the President of Tunisia pinned a medal on Jim for the humanitarian work the Forrestal had provided.

With the carrier in the Athens harbor between at-sea periods, we were able to see the country together. As always, Jim was uneasy when he was away from his command, but we tucked good Greek food and wine under our belts and learned about this remarkable country's history and its people.

Walking on the beach one evening with my husband, I stepped in a hole and hurt my foot. By morning, it was obvious it was a break, not just a sprain. The ship's schedule called for a sea deployment with a Barcelona port call and Jim was due to leave in two hours. He called down to George, who appeared at the door and when I showed him my black and swollen foot, George hurried into the bathroom and returned with a bar of soap. We finally convinced him that there was something more seriously wrong and he ran downstairs to call a cab to take me to the Air Force Hospital. A worried Jim drove to Fleet Landing, turned in the rental car and sailed away.

Enveloped in a cast to my knee, with crutches in each hand, I packed and began my journey to Barcelona with the wives. In Lucerne, Switzerland, where we changed planes and prepared for a long wait due to weather conditions, the airport authorities separated me from the others. I was firmly seated in a wheelchair, then whisked to a room where I was strip- searched and thin pieces of metal were inserted between my skin and the plaster cast on my leg. Satisfied I was not carrying contraband of any kind, they left me alone in the room, took my crutches and locked the door. It was several hours before I was even given a glass of water. The Swiss are very thorough people.

Gazing out the window at the Lucerne countryside, I realized my sight was blurry. Months before in Norfolk, I had visited the Naval Dispensary for a routine eye exam and was told after much testing, there was a degenerative disease in the backs of both eyes. The doctors were guarded in their assessment and agreed that it would not get any better, only worse and I could tell from their attitude, I was in a lot of trouble.

I didn't have time for this.

Joining Jim and traveling alone through Europe, along with my wits, I needed all my senses, and chose at that moment to continue with my plans until I either ran into walls or fell into gutters. As time passed, I would do both, but not now.

The blurring passed. Probably due to my traumatic hours with the Swiss security.

.

Coming into the Barcelona harbor, the Forrestal had to anchor five miles out and the weather turned foul. An advance party was sent in and my instructions were to come to the ship in Jim's launch. Because of the weather, he chose not to leave, and after the Rhodes experience, it was understandable. I was well acquainted with the launch crew who appeared sympathetic but unruffled by the crutches. They handed me aboard, positioned me on the deck out of the wind and rain and we roared off into eight-foot swells. There was no suitcase to deal with. Navy rules clearly stated I could not spend the night aboard the carrier and as we plowed along, I hoped the storm would move out to sea before nightfall.

Getting aboard the Forrestal was a different matter. At sea, a narrow drop ladder, with a tiny platform at its base, hugged the side of the ship and was the only way to board. On that stormy day, two Marines stood on the small square of metal mesh. Our boat was bobbing eight feet up, then eight feet down. The coxwain judged when we would be even with the platform and on his command, the other two launch crewmen threw me to the two Marines.

I was in free flight over deep water with a cast that would have taken me to the bottom. Besides that, I had never learned how to swim.

If there is a chapter in the Marine Manual about how to catch a Captain's wife over open water, these men had read it. One caught me, tossing me over his shoulder, fireman style and the other deftly fielded both crutches as they followed along behind me. We jogged up the ladder to the deck above, where another wheelchair was waiting. The two young Marines apologized for the rough treatment, but I told them that frankly, I was having a marvelous time.

The next stop was sick bay for a look at my leg. The flight surgeon cut away the Air Force cast and replaced it with a Navy cast. Only the best for the Captain's lady.

Because of the weather, Jim remained aboard most of the time in port. I sat in his stateroom and either read, wrote to the children or worked on my needlepoint. Sitting quietly in a corner of the big couch at the far end of the room, I learned a great deal about this floating city he commanded. If a man was sent to him for Captain's Mast, I slipped into the bedroom and closed the steel door. It meant disciplinary action and whoever faced my husband for that, needed all the dignity he could muster. There were unwritten rules for me to abide by and I never questioned them.

The men called the Forrestal, the FID – First In Defense. She was commissioned in 1955 as a result of the need they discovered during the Korean war for ships to fit the new jet aircraft She served in Vietnam, nearly dying from the massive fire that threatened to consume her. She survived, was rebuilt, suffered another fire and was rebuilt again. She was a seasoned ship of war and peace and earned the great respect and fondness the men felt for her.

She was my competition.

But learning about her, I felt the same fondness for the old girl. She was valiant. As her officers came to report to Jim about their respective jobs and the men who served in the divisions under them, the term floating city took on credibility. Doctors, dentists, lawyers, a library, church, the brig (jail), ship's stores, restaurants were all part of this cohesive town of 5,000 men. Jim arranged for a boxing ring on the hanger deck, giving everybody a place to vent their anger or frustrations. It soon became as popular as the basketball court.

In each Mediterranean port of call, baseball games were arranged and a group of sailors found an orphanage in Athens that needed major reconstruction. They made the repairs, repainted it, top to bottom, then returned to play with the children after the job was completed. Men at sea miss their children. Career counselors held regular hours, the radio/ TV station allowed the ethnic groups to tell their side of the story. Publications kept the entire ship's company aware of the world outside, and the world outside aware of the Forrestal.

I met the men who kept the great ship moving; from the engineers who tended the huge turbines to the electricians who saw to it this city had juice. During the flight operations conducted on the dependents' cruise to Rhodes, I watched the flight deck crew dodge the burning eyes of a jet's exhaust and brave death each time a plane launched and recovered. The steel cables that stretched taut across the deck to stop the screaming jets as they landed, had been known to snap from the strain of arresting and holding a plane. When that happened, men either died or lost their legs in the space of a second. The name for

223

these men were 'Roof Rats', and they were respected by everyone, particularly the pilots. I personally considered their jobs the most dangerous of all on the ship, with the exception of the men who flew the planes. Having been the wife of one, I knew well the edge they lived on.

Sitting with my needlepoint, I listened to the ship-wide intercom announce fire drills, flight quarters drills, man overboard drills, aircraft injury drills. Although some of these drills could only be conducted at sea, the announcements were clear testimony to the readiness of the entire ship at all times. This mobile airfield never slept.

When the carrier left Barcelona for Palma, Mallorca, most of the wives chose to follow. I took one extra day and with a crutch under each arm, stumped around the Gut, chatting with shopkeepers I had met before.

Waiting for my plane to Palma, a couple approached me and introduced themselves. The husband was a retired American Naval officer. They had heard about the Skipper's wife whose next destination was Palma. The crutches had become my label. Hannah Devlin asked if I had made arrangements for a place to stay. When I told her I would take care of that in the Palma airport, she invited me to be their guest in their home until the ship came in. I was not only amazed at their unquestioning hospitality, but grateful for their kind offer. We flew together, got acquainted, discovering we knew many of the same people in the Navy.

"Pat, did you by any chance bring a long dress with you?" There was a half smile on her face.

"Matter of fact, Hannah, I did. Can't imagine why with these wooden sticks, but it was habit, I guess."

"Good. Tomorrow night is the Lion Club's Charter Day dinner and we want you to come along with us. If you're not too tired."

I was not too tired.

Hannah's small, compact form weaved in and out as she introduced me around to a large gathering of Americans who had retired to the island of Mallorca to live. She told me her father had been a high-ranking Admiral in the German Navy during World War II, and her pride in him and love for him were very evident. Tom, her husband could have been Peter O'Toole's twin..

My dinner partner was a retired Air Force officer and one of the founders of this Lion Club chapter. He explained he was alone because his wife was in the hospital, ill with a bleeding ulcer. His concern bordered on desperation. She had an unusual blood type and they had gathered all that was available on the island.

"I need to get her back to the States, but she would never survive the trip without the blood she needs."

I felt a funny tingle on the back of my neck. "What is her blood type?"

He had rested his forehead on the palm of his hand.. "B positive. But there's none left in Mallorca."

I stretched out my arm and said, "Yes, there is. Where do I go to do this?"

Next morning, I was driven to the hospital and gave enough blood to get his wife back to Jacksosnville, Florida.

On the return flight to Athens, I changed planes in Rome and a baggage porter stole all of my jewelry out of my train case as the ticket agent kept my attention with a pointless argument about my ticket. Six months later, they broke the ring of thieves, including the ticket agents, but my pretties were gone.

The wives -- all one hundred twenty-one of them -- who had come to Athens to be near their husbands, were staunch. They bent with the wind and some of the breezes were quite stiff. One girl went home with tuberculosis, one with spinal meningitis. Living conditions were not the best. Heat in the winter was in short supply in this resort town and milk was not refrigerated. Some had their children with them and that carried its own set of problems. Most of the wives lived in Glyfada, so we met often in the Congo Palace, a hotel across from my apartment building. Usually, the word on the ship's arrival came to me first and with advance notice, we were able to be in whatever port the ship was anchored. I admired these women and their unfailing capacity to adjust. When they trouped off to Sicily, I remained behind. The ship's visit was a brief one and I knew Jim would be too busy to find time for me.

One of the wives rented a car and with another wife, was on her way to their hotel. Waiting at a stoplight, a man on a motorcycle threw a brick through her window, grabbed the purse that was on her lap and roared off. She spent her time in Sicily in a hospital, having her face put back together.

These were gutsy women who had made hard decisions in order to be with their husbands. Their priorities were carved out of months of living alone; not once, but on a routine basis while their husbands fulfilled their commitment to their job and their country. They had lives 'back home', easier lives, more comfortable lives with continuity and security for themselves and their children, but the natural order of any marriage is familiarity with the person you live with and that, they did not have because of the continual separations.

At four o'clock one morning, my phone rang. It was Ruthie, an Air Wing wife whose husband had flown off the ship and into Athens on some official errand. He would be there only a few hours, then leave at dawn to return to the Forrestal. Ruthie had a problem.

"Pat, I know it's a terrible time to call. I'm sorry if I woke you up, but Terry flew in tonight and he's here in our apartment with me now."

Groggy, I answered, "Lucky you."

"Pat, we don't know what to do. The waterbed in my apartment sits on the marble floor and it's too cold to sleep on. I've been sleeping on the couch because of the weather, but it's not wide enough for both of us."

Short of offering my double bed, I knew I had to come up with an answer. "Ruthie, go fill the bathtub with hot water, light a few candles and give Terry a night to remember."

There was a long pause, an intake of breath, then a giggle. "Thanks Pat. I knew you'd think of something." She sounded hurried and I was left with a dial tone.

My relationship with our children was long distance and frustrating. Midway through the cruise, Jamey wrote she was expecting her second baby. She promised to keep me informed of her progress and knowing how far away Athens was from California, she didn't ask me to come. It was a hard time for me. I needed to be with my daughter when she had her baby, yet distance, cost and the official duties of a Commanding Officer's wife in foreign countries also had their demands. As it turned out, my second granddaughter was born before I even knew of it. With the ship due at some future date to make port in Naples, friends had asked me to house-sit while he reported to Wiesbaden, Germany for two weeks of briefings. It gave me a place to live, but the NATO communications in Naples had no idea where I was when the message came in. It was days before I learned that all was well with my daughter and her baby. Two months later, when the cruise ended and I returned to Norfolk, I boarded the next plane to California and had a belated introduction to my new granddaughter, Ashli.

Jeff's year was one of hard work. Holding down two jobs and monitoring classes at the University of Texas left him little time to miss anything but sleep. The fall would find him registering to resume his college career, but I would be there for summer vacation if he had one. Because our children had grown up in this environment they knew nothing else. For Jim and me, our constant separations demanded togetherness whenever there was a chance for it. Once again, I was torn between children and husband with the Navy's unrelenting demands.

Patricia Linder

CHAPTER TWENTY FIVE

July 1973

At the end of the ten-month cruise, the Forrestal returned to Norfolk. Four months later, it turned around and went back to the Mediterranean.

So did I.

The interim summer months were spent visiting the children. Jeff, looking like he could use it, came for some home cooking and family renewal. My trip to California to see Jamey's new baby established me as the Flying Grandmother and I basked in the warmth of normal family life.

Jim's name was on the screening list for the rank of Rear Admiral.

Twenty-five years went into that. Although there were further grades of flag rank to aspire to, making Admiral was momentous. The word came as the ship was returning from an at sea period in the Caribbean., before leaving for the Med. Good friends like to pass along good news and my phone rang steadily for two days before the Forrestal nosed into its berth at the Norfolk Naval Station.

As I walked along the dock, leading the ladies to the Quarterdeck ladder and the signal to board, I spotted Jim. Close to my chest, I gave him a 'thumbs up' signal, not knowing if he knew. He pretended he didn't understand, but I caught his smile.

He knew.

We didn't light any fireworks. So much had gone into the past twenty-five years, it was more a time of remembrance and assessment. The children were delighted and proud of their father and I had one more answer to 'was it worth it?' Orders would follow, but we both assumed it would be Washington again. In the Navy's eyes, with the Sylvania command, followed immediately by command of the carrier Forrestal, Jim had spent three full years having fun. And he did. On our massive new coffee table, embedded with the ship's seal and the nine Air Wing squadron insignias., his Wardroom Officers, who had planned and executed the gift had these words engraved on the brass plate in the lower right hand corner:

CAPTAIN JAMES B. LINDER, USN
"THE 'PEOPLE' CAPTAIN WHO DID IT RIGHT THE
FIRST TIME AND HAD FUN DOING IT"
COMMANDING OFFICER – NOVEMBER 1972 – MAY 1974

The past three years were probably the best time of his life, yet I saw new lines etched in his face, the sprinkling of gray at his temples. He was still tall and arrow straight, the weight of responsibility had not bowed his shoulders, but it had laid its mark on the set of his jaw and the intensity of his gaze. His powers of concentration were even more focused than they were before. Our family joke with an edge was the reminder that my name was Pat.

The coming Mediterranean cruise meant that Jim would depart with the Forrestal, but give up his ship to the next Captain in four months. It was then that he would put on the stars and braid of his new rank. .

February 1974

The big yellow bag found its way to Goodwill and smaller, lighter ones were purchased. Experience had taught me many things during those years of living from pillar to post. I enjoyed the familiarity of the various foreign airports and felt like a seasoned traveler. Independence had become essential in order to survive the intricacies of hotel reservations, flight schedules, money and the personal assurance I could take care of myself.

The ship's first port of call was Cannes, France on our Fourth of July. General de Gaulle, whose dislike of the United States and Great Britain kept U.S. ships from visiting that country, had made his final departure in early 1970 and the U S Fleet was welcome, once again. I flew in with the wife of the Forrestal's navigator. She looked like a miniature Elizabeth Taylor and with her sparkling eyes, cloud of black hair and deep chuckle, we sailed through the trip to Europe with ease. Cannes was spread out before us like a brand new dress. The ship was due in the next day and because Jim had said "The Carlton", we found the magnificent hotel, checked in and entered our high - ceilinged suite with French doors that opened out onto a balcony over-looking the French Riviera. The furniture was exquisite, flowers on every table and a large bowl of fruit. Assuming our husbands had made the arrangements, we sighed deeply, thinking what dears they were to treat us to such luxury. Faustina headed for the marble bathtub in a room the size of our living room at home.

I gazed at the beauty of the beach and the blue Mediterranean as she splashed about, then wandered to the door that had the room rate posted. When I asked her to translate francs to dollars, she came shooting out of the bathroom, wrapped in a towel.

"My God. Jack will have a heart attack when he finds out what this costs."

I had my doubts about the condition of Jim's blood pressure when he arrived and realized the astronomical amount he would be paying.

There was a knock on the door. Faustina and I looked at each other. She fled for the bathroom and summoning as much dignity as I could, I opened it to find the ship's advance officer on the other side.

"Hello, Pat. The Captain sent me on ahead to make arrangements for the crew and to see if you found your room." Tom's eyes shifted to peer over my shoulder into the room and on out to the balcony. The expression on his face was one of complete disbelief, bewilderment, then panic. "Did you request this room?"

"No Tom. We checked in, they looked us up on the reservation list and brought us here. I don't know who made the reservations, but did anybody check the price?"

Tom's face was the color of the calla lilies in the vase on the table. "I called and asked for a room for the Forrestal's Commanding Officer's lady and her companion. I thought the clerk sounded a little impressed."

"Well, much as I could get used to this, Jim would have to float a loan to stay here." I could see the end of my hour of luxury.

Tom had entered the room, and when I showed him the rates, his eyes closed in disbelief and pain.

"I'll be right back. Don't go away." And he fled. Go away, indeed. They would have to remove me at gunpoint.

Twenty minutes later, Faustina and I found ourselves in two rather pleasant, little rooms done up in chintz in the back of the hotel. This was reality. Our moment of glory had ended. The upside was she would not have to worry about Jack's heart and I need not be concerned about Jim's blood pressure. However, I felt like someone's poor relation.

Three days later, Jim and I were to attend a ceremony to be held on the roof of the Cannes Film Festival building. In his white uniform, full medals and the white hat with the 'scrambled eggs' on the brim, he looked quite handsome and official. I was unaware of the reason for the ceremony and was questioning him as we started up the long, narrow flight of steps leading to the dignitaries waiting for us by the front doors.

Without warning, a crowd of hippies raced up the steps, grabbed Jim's hat, pushing him as they milled around us. They threw the hat to each other and realizing he was in danger, I began flailing at stringy-haired heads with my purse. In the melee that followed, I intercepted Jim's hat just as the gendarmes suddenly appeared and with wooden sticks, clubbed the members of the mob, sending them rolling down the steep stairs. There was a paddy wagon waiting at the bottom and they were loaded in, disappearing around a corner, with siren hooting. We resumed our march up the steep steps as though nothing had happened. It was over so quickly, I wondered if it really had.

The French dignitaries by the doors were horrified and apologized profusely, trying to make sure we were not injured. One mentioned American hippies, but it was later discovered the leader of the pack was the son of a member of the French parliament.

On the roof, we were ushered to chairs surrounded by more chairs containing elderly French men and women. There wasn't an official among them. Their expressions were benign and the plump ladies looked like loving grandmothers. Jim had not had time to brief me on what this was, so I shook the fragile hands held out to me and settled into my chair to listen to the words of description being spoken and translated.

I was dumfounded. These dear old souls had served in the French Underground during the Second World War. They were responsible for the safe escapes of countless British and American airmen, shot down by the Germans in France. On this day, they would receive medals for their brave exploits and listening to descriptions of their heroism, I was appalled and thrilled at the chances they took to protect and move the pilots trying to get back to England. One sweet-faced lady in her seventies, with dimpled cheeks as pink as apples, had killed several of the enemy in order to obey her instructions

General de Gaulle had refused to allow these heroes to be recognized because of his dislike for the Americans and British. Now that he was dead, the medals were ceremoniously pinned on each chest and bosom. I felt honored to be included in something so meaningful and as I shook each hand, I tried to tell them of my admiration and gratitude. Because of one Frenchman's snit, it had taken twenty-eight years.

Since it was our Fourth of July, and the Forrestal was the first American ship to enter Cannes, fireworks lighted the sky and a spectacular show followed with dancing girls from the Folies Bergere in Paris. The Casino hosted the wonderful evening and I no longer felt like the poor relative. We were met with genuine joy and hospitality at our presence in France. American and French flags flew side by side.

Sitting at a sidewalk café on a sun-drenched afternoon some days later, we discussed my itinerary for the next two weeks. The ship would slide out to sea and I knew I must pick a place to light. Genoa by train came to mind. It was on the way to Naples, the ship's next port of call and the Genoa run was one of the most breathtaking trips in Europe because of the many tunnels, high mountains and flashes of the Mediterranean.

Friends who were with the American Embassy in Paris and in Cannes for the festivities, joined us. As so often happened, they asked me to be their guest. Skip knew the ship's schedule, discussed it with his wife and they decided to extend the invitation.

Paris. I would go to Paris. It was a woman's city and I was a woman. With Jim's sanction, arrangements were made. Skip and Cathy planned to leave Cannes the following morning and I would follow on the train in two days when the ship was scheduled to leave.

Our friends met me in the Paris train station and we drove to their apartment one block from the Champs Elysees. This was probably as close to heaven as I would ever come and I determined not to waste a moment of the week. That night, Skip and Cathy introduced me to the Metro system, we strolled the Left Bank, listened to the guitars on the steps of Montmartre and I reveled in the Pigalle. This was my kind of place.

Putting a fistful of subway tokens in my hand, Skip presented an itinerary the Embassy had made for me, with trips to Versailles, Le Petit Trianon and other places familiar and favored by tourists. I chose what appealed and discarded the rest. My subway tokens took me to the outskirts of Paris to the Baccarat Crystal Museum and I spent an afternoon with Catherine the Great's chandelier .It was in great need of a good dusting.

A couturier fashion show was being offered by Coco Chanel. I had a ticket. A Parisian beauty salon gave me a 'do'. The Tuilleries, the Champs Elysees, Le Drug Store, the Arc de Triomphe and the Louvre, they were mine for a week. I no longer felt capable, I felt female. Paris re-established my femininity. The hauling of heavy suitcases faded at the sight of the Luxembourg Gardens. I met smiles with my own. It was still too early for the chestnut trees to be in bloom, but it didn't matter. I was in bloom.

Yet, every dream has an ending and I caught the plane to Naples in time to be on Fleet Landing when the Forrestal appeared like a silent, gray ghost on the horizon.

CHAPTER TWNETY SIX

The next few months were spent criss-crossing the Mediterranean, following the ship. I was the Navy equivalent of a camp follower, the only things I lacked were the pots and pans. .I felt like the greyhound, chasing the mechanical rabbit. My official name was Seagull.

Naples still had its sights and sounds of laughter, but Athens was changed now because of the political posture of the new government. I no longer found the people as friendly. After the military coup, the US was in disfavor because of our Turkish connections. A déjà vu visit to Glyfada brought fewer smiles this time and I felt sadness at the perfidy of people I had thought were my friends. Before, a Greek family had included us in their Easter celebration, more sacred to them than any other religious holiday. That day, we played games with the children, were given hard-boiled eggs dyed red that had special meaning. We shared their food, met their family and left them knowing the day would be remembered by all. It was only a year later, but the political doctrine was not a friendly one and we did not wish to put them in an embarrassing position.

The short trips Jim and I took together, shopping for flokati rugs, eating squid and drinking the Greek retsina wine, belied the seriousness of the Forrestal's presence in that NATO country. One evening, Jim returned from the ship with a set jaw. He had learned that members of the Black September terrorist group had been training in Australia for several months; their target – the Forrestal – to be blown out of the water by extensive underwater demolition. The

239

end result was almost ludicrous, if not tragic. While arming their bombs in a Pirreus hotel room, they blew themselves and a good portion of the hotel to dust. Always, there is the undercurrent of violence in a 'peaceful mission'.

The ship left at night for Palma. It was unnerving to see its silhouette on the horizon in the afternoon of one day and nothing, the next. American aircraft carriers had been called 'the big sticks', and when Teddy Roosevelt coined the phrase, "Speak softly and carry a big stick", that was precisely what it was about. Some NATO countries needed the example of might as their protector because of their small or antiquated navies. The carrier in the outlying waters of such a country was a symbol of peace as well as force.

.In nearly every port, Jim scheduled a Marine Review. It was always held at sunset with the ship swung at anchor to frame the city in the immense opening of the hanger-bay, flight deck elevator. Like a gigantic TV screen, the great space provided a breathtaking sight. The city's dignitaries were invited and following the review, a buffet supper was served. The galley cooked quantities of unusual and appealing food that was served on long tables with linen cloths. There was never a crumb or a crust left.

The Review itself, began with the guests being seated in the hanger bay, facing the elevator opening. The ship's Navy band played until sunset. At that time, with the first measured notes of the *Star Spangled Banner,* the elevator began its slow descent from the flight deck. As it moved down, the audience watched as the Marine Drill Team came into view in the center, flanked by Marines lining its outer edge. Each man held a large flag, representing one of the different NATO countries. As the elevator slammed into place, the Drill Team marched off to the center of the deck in front of the guests. For a quarter of an hour, close order silent drill followed with guns flying through the air. No music, just the sound of the guns as the men caught them and performed the pre-firing mechanics.

To say it was impressive is an understatement. The precision, discipline and potential power of that close knit group, left no question in the minds of the people watching,, that these Marines and the ship they lived on, were a force to be reckoned with. I always felt a visceral jolt of pride at every performance.

Often, I served as hostess to Jim's guests at luncheons while the ship was in port. The menus were submitted to him by his stewards, choices made and the flowers for the table were my responsibility. If a wife was accompanying her husband, I was expected to know the best places for all kinds of shopping and dining. This was an important demonstration of American good will. An aircraft carrier is a weapon of war, but the people who man it also have the capacity of friendship that signifies peace.

Depending on the amount of time the ship was in port, we lived around the necessary obligations and snatched as much time together as possible. Sometimes, there was little or none. An aircraft carrier is an unusual thing to have in your front yard and there was always an endless procession of security- cleared nationals who couldn't wait to visit. It was good international relations and a boost for the morale of the ship's complement and the Air Wing.

The Forrestal was due for a lengthy time at sea and I boarded a plane to Geneva, spent a few days as a tourist, then on to Rome to do more of the same. My ultimate destination was Naples.

Wandering about Europe was not easy. It was tiring. There was always the luggage and the hassle of dealing with unfamiliar languages. I was never in a country long enough to become fluent in any of them and around the Mediterranean, the similarities added to the confusion. By using my hands and facial expressions, I could make my way, but it was exhausting. I felt tattered from packing and unpacking. My clothes never looked crisp or completely clean.

My trip to Paris had rejuvenated me, but I was looking forward to the end. I missed my own country. With no radio to tune into the Armed Forces station, I was completely out of touch. When the ship was in port, Jim often gave me a printed encapsulated version of the daily news. The publications department supplied it to all aboard, but when I was on the wing, my only source was the one newspaper in the English language that carried more European news than American, and was not always available.

Simply put, I was homesick, not just for my children and my home, but for my country.

May 1973

From Naples, Jim took the Forrestal to Athens as his final port of call. His Change of Command would be held on the hanger deck and the reception would follow at the Hilton Hotel in downtown Athens. His new orders read that he was to report to the Defense Department,

Washington, D.C. to become the Director of Administration for the Navy.

A message came through during the night, changing the plans. The ship was ordered to depart a few hours after the ceremony, due to a problem somewhere in the Med. Without hesitation, Plan B kicked in and following the official part of the command change, Jim's officers and the Admirals who had come to participate, moved to the Officers' Wardroom for the reception. It was there that my husband changed his Captain's coat and hat for ones bearing the braid and insignia of Flag Rank. I carried them to the visiting Admiral who was the speaker for the Change of Command and he held the coat for Jim to shrug into. Besides the unfamiliar braid on his new coat, my husband took on a different look.

An hour later, after saying goodbye to his officers and men, we boarded his launch and looking back for a final wave, discovered that neither of us could speak.

I would miss the gray mistress, too.

At the Hilton, after changing into more comfortable clothes, we caught a cab to Pirreus for a late lunch at a favorite taverna on the sea. Our twenty-fifth wedding anniversary would be in June and our gift to each other was a ten-day cruise around the Greek Islands. For Jim, it ws a busman's holiday, but there were still places we had missed and this was an answer to that.

At the tiny restaurant in Pirreus, Jim rented the little blue rowboat and talked its owner into rowing us out to the Forrestal for his last inspection.

When we returned to the Hilton, we slipped into the bar for a toast.   A lot had happened that day and it was appropriate to acknowledge the bitter with the sweet. Seated at a table, Jim called my attention to a man leaning slumped, on the bar at the far end of the room. He rose and walked to the man, said a few words and the two of them returned to our table.   I was introduced to Spiro Agnew, the past Vice President of the United States. Watergate had ended, Nixon was gone and Mr. Agnew was out of a job. He had been unsuccessful in cashing a check at the hotel desk, and since we were staying there, Jim offered to take care of it for him. He left for a brief time and returned with the money.

For over an hour, Mr. Agnew spoke with us, telling the other side of the story and adding, "Perhaps not in my lifetime, but sometime in the future, historians will tell the true story of Watergate. It's not the same story that was told by the press and media."   Yet, he was philosophical about the end result, taking full responsibility for his part in the sad affair.

As we sat listening to this Greek-American bear of a man, young Americans filtered into the bar. When they spotted Mr. Agnew, they came to our table and asked to shake his hand. He was overwhelmed. At least a dozen times, he rose to his fee to take an outstretched hand. When at last, he rose to go, he thanked us both, inviting us to visit him in the US when we returned.

Congratulating Jim one more time on his new promotion, he said, "I'm going around to tell each one of those young people how much it has meant to me to be recognized by them."   And he did. It was a different man who, with shoulders straight, strode out of the Hilton bar.

Patricia Linder

CHAPTER TWENTY SEVEN

May 1974

Our tour of duty in Washington, D.C. lasted one short year. We had rented our house in Virginia Beach, packed up and moved into a McLean, Virginia three -story townhouse.

We settled in, Jim reported to the Pentagon and I cast about for something to do. Washington had gone through the firestorm of Watergate and on television, I watched Richard Nixon say goodbye to his Presidency as Gerald Ford stepped into the job.

The war in Vietnam slogged on.

While I was living in Greece in 1973, the Prisoners of War had been released on January 12th. It was a day of deep satisfaction for me, but bitter sweet because of the more than 2,000 men still listed as MIA, Missing in Action. The war itself would not end until April 20th 1975. The evacuation of Saigon and the resulting fall of South Vietnam to the northern forces, made that terrible war completely pointless.

For the first time in the history of our young country, we retreated and gave up the fight. To a professional military man, defeat has an acid taste. To the wives and families who lost husbands, sons or fathers, it was gut-wrenching, the only compensation being that they had served their country with honor and without question. Packing away a husband's clothes and the things that bind a man and woman together, only leaves a shattering emptiness in its wake. Many of the wives of the MIAs would not remarry, but continue on for years, the struggle to find any indication of what happened to their men.

Washington duty means it's 'in your face'. After three years of absence from the American media, I found the onslaught of words, pictures and opinions more of an assault than entertainment or enlightenment. In the Mediterranean, I had missed having news of my country, but this was offensive. To be a public servant meant swimming around in a tank of sharks. I wondered if Watergate's legacy would be one of mediocrity.

I needed a job. And found it with a research council that dealt with labor union violations in the public sector. It sounded dull, but the lesson learned was, you don't mess around with the upper echelons of labor unions. They play dirty. To make a sensitive phone call for my boss, I had to leave the building and find a pay phone because my desk was bugged. Still, with that always in mind, I enjoyed learning about something new to my experience.

Frequent trips to the Bethesda Naval Hospital only confirmed the original diagnosis on my eyes and proved that doctors really don't want to see someone they can't fix. I continually adjusted my life to one of less sight and cursed the gods for my tribulation. But I didn't spend a lot of time on it.

Jim, as Director of Administration, was Pentagon desk-bound and it was no wonder he was relieved, if not elated to be told he had 'screened' for command of a Battle Group. In just eleven short months, we packed up and moved back to Norfolk into Quarters on the Naval Air Station.

May 1975

It was my first time to live in Quarters. The house was red brick, solid as the South, two story with five bedrooms, a corresponding number of bathrooms and nobody but me to take care of it. Stewards were in short supply and assigned only to the higher- ranking Admirals, at home and at sea. I turned the servant's room off the kitchen into a cozy TV nest, spending most of my time there when Jim was gone. And Jim was gone most of the time.

A Battle Group Command consists of an aircraft carrier, a cruiser and four destroyers with an increased amount of personnel and responsibility. The carrier that would house Jim during the next two years was the USS America. It was his Flagship – where he lived when he was with his Command. During NATO exercises involving those countries' navies, Jim's command would grow to include other ships, and at any given time he could have the responsibility of the safety of seven to eight thousand people -- U.S. and foreign.

There were furrows in his brow and a tenseness that didn't go away. His mind was always on something else or somewhere else and I began to dread the times alone. Thank God for television and good books. Because of my intent to follow him again for the two years he was designated to keep the job, I chose not to work. Visiting the children and catching up on our families filled the first few months, but that ended as we all returned to our lives and I was once again left standing at the window, staring at whatever was out there.

The phone rang early one Monday morning and a friend in Washington whom I had met during my days on Roger Zion's Staff, called to see what I was doing. Olive Hunt had worked for a Congressman from Tennessee and was a very savvy lady.

"In answer to your question, I'm doing nothing and going crackers in the process. There's a lot of green grass out there and I feel like I know every blade personally,"

"Standing at the window again?" She knew me well. "Has Jim left?"

"That he has and it's the Caribbean. It's a different kind of duty, Olive. He's mostly at sea with an occasional weekend at home, but not often, and he'll be leaving one of these days for another long cruise in the Med."

"Will you be following along?"

"Of course, but until then, I'm at loose ends."

Olive Hunt from Tennessee became my salvation.

"Dearie, I'm working in the White House and they need a volunteer. You could stay with me at my house in the Tennessee suite in the basement. We'll go in together and come home together and you can drive back to Norfolk for the weekend. What do you say?"

"Is a thundering YES good enough?" I was already reaching for my car keys. "Jim's gone now for two weeks and it only takes me four hours to drive to Washington."

"Good. I'll have your clearance and ID in the mill by the time you get here and you can begin work tomorrow morning." She sounded as pleased as I was excited.

We arranged to meet at a place familiar to us both. With the skills I had learned in Europe, I packed in fifteen minutes flat and called my neighbor to alert her of my sporadic absences. Phoning the wife of Jim's Aide, I promised she would get my Washington phone number as soon as I knew it. Nancy was my strong right hand. She was a talented and lovely blonde girl from Texas with two young redheaded sons who had become like our own as we shared the past few months together.

All that remained was to close up the house and drive to Washington. And I could do it with a clear conscience. With this tour of duty, I had little responsibility for the wives. Each ship handled their own domestic problems and Jim's command came with a Staff that took care of itself. For the first time in twenty-six years, I felt like a free agent. Missing was the easy camaraderie of the Forrestal wives, but all things change.

What a romp. Olive's office was in the Executive Office Building across the street from the West Wing. The jobs she had lined up were fascinating and demanding.

I was a volunteer assistant to Pamela Powell, director of youth programs for the Ford Administration. I also served on the staff that made the arrangements for President Ford's trips.

Pam answered her phone one morning, talked for a while, obviously to someone she cared about, then said, "Mom, my other line is waiting for me, so talk to my assistant for a minute while I take care of it." She handed me the phone.

A husky, very familiar voice said, "Hello, you on the other end of the line. How are you?"

I was talking to the movie star June Allyson.

Pam Powell was the daughter of June Allyson and Dick Powell, another movie star popular in the forties. It was a good conversation and reluctantly, I turned over the phone to Pam when she finished her other call.

I shuttled back and forth between the two offices and if there was a call for a warm body in the White House Rose Garden for a presentation, the honor was mine. Henry Kissinger frequently came out of his office, walking the short distance to the Oval Office. President Ford, with his benign smile, gave speeches and patted small heads if the Scouts were there to present an award. The roses smelled good and I felt like I had fallen into a bed of them.

Late on Friday afternoon, if Jim was coming in, I left the White House and drove to Norfolk. Monday mornings found me on the road north as soon as he left for the ship. One perk that came with the job was an official car to take him back and forth, so I no longer had to drop him off and watch him leave. Seeing the back end of a ship as it departs the pier is a not-so-exquisite form of punishment for a wife.

All good things come to an end and Battle Group Four made ready for another trip to the Mediterranean. I reluctantly said goodbye to my White House friends, was given a bracelet charm indicating President Ford's appreciation and made the drive to Norfolk for the last time.

Jim left and after closing up the Quarters,, so did I. My suitcases looked well-used and had developed the character that only airlines know how to bestow. Looking at the clouds below me as the plane sped toward Naples, I missed the churning excitement of my first time over the Atlantic. So much had happened in the interim – Vietnam, Washington, three other cruises, more Washington. Each had left its unique mark on my personality and I thought about the things learned. I was richer for the experience, but the price of this life was one of continual loneliness. My accomplishments were the result of living alone. Yet, I had to question my ability to spend every day of my life in the same place, with the same people and wait for the problems that would inevitably come. My parents had done that and done it well. I doubted my attempt at such a life would be as successful. There's nothing like a window seat to turn one philosophical.

Patricia Linder

CHAPTER TWENTY EIGHT

Italy, 1975

An apartment was waiting for me in Naples when I arrived. Jim's Aide, David had tracked one down and part of the deal was a Volkswagen Bug parked in the front courtyard. I had never driven one, but when Jim flew into Naples for a meeting, he called me from the airport with the good news he would be in Naples overnight. Never having driven a Bug before, I put it in gear, crept up my perpendicular street and discovered I was a Neapolitan driver. Instinctively, avoiding all eye contact, I drove on the sidewalk if necessary and gave the proper hand signals that would either get me to my destination, or start a riot. Driving Jim back to the apartment left him white as a sheet and almost speechless, but we made it. I doubt he was ever that terrified, flying off a carrier.

Jim was a very busy man. His Battle Group was part of the Sixth Fleet in the Mediterranean and involved in NATO exercises. He flew into Naples whenever there was a meeting that required his presence. Although the carrier, America was now his Flagship, he missed the stimulation of driving his own ship, but the demands on him were more serious and intense.

He also had an edge. During his command of the Forrestal, it was home to another Admiral, thereby making it a Flagship. For two years, Jim had the chance to observe the correlation between the two commands and by doing so, was familiar with its intricacies.

Patricia Linder

1975 The Meditteranean

During The Lebanon Civil War, Battle Group Four was ordered into eastern Mediterranean waters. A large number of non-Lebanese refugees, Americans as well as other nationalities, and their families were caught in Beirut and it was up to Jim and his fleet of ships to evacuate them. Russian submarines tailed them as they moved across the Med and our submarines followed the Russians.

I knew of this order because of a friend in Naples. Jim had been at sea when the messages came in and the Battle Group immediately formed up and headed east. Chuck Williams called to tell me there would be a delay in his arrival date back in Naples. Lebanon was in the news, and the grapevine had it we were involved. It wasn't difficult to put two and two together.

Some delay. As they steamed toward the coast of Lebanon, Russian ships surrounded them with missiles poised for launch. Arab nationals with rapid-fire, automatic weapons lined the waterfront.

Half of the fleeing people in Beirut had left that city by bus for Damascus. Embassy personnel were among the passengers and they had no escort. Planes on the carrier America were armed and ready to provide air cover for the buses in case of attacks. But an order came down to disarm the aircraft. The rebels had demanded the planes fly only over water and would not be allowed over land for the duration of the bus trip.

The other refugees streamed aboard the liberty boats sent in to take them to the waiting ships. Once loaded, the Fleet turned toward Greece.

Turkey, the closest country was no longer friendly. The U.S. had imposed an embargo on military aid to that country because of the stalemate between Turkey and Greece over Cyprus. In retaliation, Turkey seized our military bases located within their borders. The Greek government, once again our friends, indicated they would allow the refugees to disembark in Athens. The word for this is 'geopolitics'.

Mission accomplished, the Fleet turned toward Naples and began its run. Midway there, it was discovered that some of the evacuees offloaded in Greece had immediately gone back to Beirut on any transport they could find.

To get their cars and their pets.

Once again, orders were issued and Battle Group Four reversed course and steamed into enemy waters to evacuate the same people and their pets -- one more time. Their cars were left behind.

It was all very hush, hush, but when Jim returned, there was no missing the fire in his eyes. He had seen the men on board his ships put in harm's way by a few thoughtless people.

Keeping to the schedule, despite the Lebanon crisis, the Fleet sailed to Rhodes for an official visit. Jim had meetings with the mayor of the city and his itinerary left little time for us to see each other. I opted to remain in Naples.

Good decision.

When the America anchored off Rhodes, Jim, in full uniform, with his Chief of Staff were flown by helicopter to the island with the understanding that the Admiral's barge would be waiting at the pier to return them to the ship. An unfriendly crowd was waiting to see an American Admiral come onto their island. They were Rhodes' communists and the mood was ugly.

Jim and his Chief of Staff were taken by official car to the Parliament Building where he joined the dignitaries inside. The growing crowd had followed and rocks began to fly. As the tall windows were broken out by the angry mob, the two men positioned themselves between the windows to escape the flying glass. The Greek dignitaries fled.

It became obvious that little would be accomplished in the way of meetings and with unanimous consent, Jim made the decision to return to his Flagship. The two men ran out the back of the building, hailed a cab and returned to the airport. The crowd's attention turned to the barge crew at the pier and as rocks pelted them, they took the big launch out to sea and back to the ship. They had been alerted to the danger and knew the Admiral would fly back to the America. As they pulled away, a rock hit the coxswain, injuring him. It was not a successful day of diplomacy. Rhodes, being Greek but close to the Turkish coast, was more violent in their protests against the United States than the Greek people on the mainland.

All of this over the island of Cyprus. Some months later on April of 1976, the United States solved the situation by giving Turkey one billion dollars in military and economic aid and Greece, seven hundred million dollars. We were all friends again. And as the Greek cruise ship captain had said, "Don't wait around for a thank you."

June 1976

Orders were due.   Battle Group Four would soon be turned over to the next man and once again, our lives were changing.   The previous two years had been ones of constant separations.   There was so little of Jim.   Our times together were like film in fast forward.   I could only sit back and wait for the crumbs of his time.   I traveled with the wives, seeing a lot of Europe, but often feeling like a widow out with the girls.

I suppose he was no different from any other good man in a like position, but with the so-called irrationality of a woman, that didn't cut it.   Simply put, I was tired of his being 'operational'.   Twenty-eight years of fits and starts had worn me down and I felt disillusionment setting in. I missed the warm feelings of affection that had been such a part of our earlier years.   With so many separations, his returns had always meant the excitement of renewed feelings. Now, my 'other life' of living without him had become my reality.   It would have been so easy to fall back on *"I don't care"*, but too much of that and your life, whatever it is, loses its meaning. Wondering if the next set of orders would put us where we could catch up on our marriage, I listened as Jim broke the news.   Aware I was getting prickly about a lot of things, he was on his best behavior when he smiled sweetly and, as if handing me the Taj Mahal, said, "How do you feel about going to China? I have orders to Taiwan."

Taiwan was a dubious label in the back of a sweater. I didn't even know where Taiwan was. Or why, after seven years in the Mediterranean, we were being sent in the opposite direction.

"It's an island in the South China Seas and it used to be called Formosa."

I was having a lesson in geography.

"I'll be the Commander of the Taiwan Defense Command and they tell me our Quarters are the best in all of Southeast Asia."

"Will there be someone there to clean the bathrooms?"

"You'll have a staff of five people."

"Will one of them clean the bathrooms?"

"I'll see to it they do."

An island with a U.S. Military Base in the middle of the South China Seas, just possibly, out of the mainstream. We would have three years of getting reacquainted. I knew it was a complicated part of the world, but Chinese politics had yet to impact on my life.

On a balmy spring day in Norfolk, as I was clearing the closets in our Quarters prior to packing the many boxes that waited for our things, the phone rang.

"Mrs. Linder? I'm with the State Department – the China desk. Are you by any chance packing for your move to Taiwan?"

Eerie. How did he know and who was he?

"I'm calling to tell you not to. I'm only trying to help you."

Click. End of call.

Of course I reported it to Jim who was as mystified as I was. But he chose to ignore it.

"Can you imagine my going to the Department of Defense and saying, "I don't think we should go to Taiwan because some anonymous guy at State called my wife and told her not to pack? They'd tell me to get the hell out the office and onto the next plane west."

Of course he was right, but why did I have this uneasy feeling? My fantasy of an idyllic time on an island began to dim.

CHAPTER TWENTY NINE

It was a half of a world away, but next to Paris, China had always been one of my favorites. My childhood was spent with Pearl Buck books and now, the mysterious Far East beckoned.

Oddly enough, instead of the usual year of cultural training given personnel before they enter a country to live for two or three years, we were given no advance information on the island or the people. Jim received military briefings, but short of an ability to use chopsticks without putting out an eye, I was fairly uninformed. Not much was written on Taiwan, previously called Formosa. Jim instructed me not to use the latter name. Generalissimo Chiang Kai-shek had renamed the island when he brought his two million Nationalist forces and their families there in 1949. They were refugees, fleeing the Chinese communists who, after a protracted war, had beaten them back to the sea.

Taiwan politics was a very complicated affair. My little bit of research before we left Norfolk told me that as Formosa, they had, down through the centuries, endured many invasions from other countries. Being in the middle of the South China Sea, with only the Straits of Taiwan separating them from Mainland China, the island was vulnerable to the many ships using that trade route.

The Taiwanese people were a meld of many cultures and when Chiang Kai-shek and his Nationalist Chinese moved there in 1949, it became the Republic of China. As I would learn during our stay in Taiwan, China took a very dim view of an island they considered theirs, splitting off to become *another* China and one with the United States as a protector. The Chinese communists on the Mainland became The Peoples' Republic of China and flexing their muscles with a threat to take back Taiwan, found us peering down their throats.

Because of the Taiwan Defense Treaty between the Republic of China (ROC) and the United States, drawn up in 1954, the Taiwan Defense Command was created. American troops and military assistance groups were sent to dig in and wave the big stick. It worked for awhile, but the China dragon to the west, periodically breathed fire and we countered with a 'visit' from the fleet.

Dimly, I recalled the newspaper coverage of the Chinese move to Taiwan, but 1949 was the year we were married and my mind simply was not on what the Chinese were doing.

It was now. We were going in an official capacity and from experience, I had to know how to behave. Operating out of ignorance in a foreign country is dicey at best. At worst, it could create an international incident.

We gathered the children in San Diego for a last reunion and loving time. China was so far away and my instincts were to stay behind and bake cookies with the granddaughters. Jeff needed new underwear and socks and I was just the person to take care of that motherly chore. He also needed feeding. How could I possibly leave this tall, slender boy-man to fend for himself. The fact that he had been doing that for the past three years, escaped my attention. I flat out, wanted more time with my children.

Not to be. But I promised him we would be there for his college graduation and sooner, whenever they let us come home. They let go and I let go, but it was harder than ever before.

July 1977

Walking into the Tokyo airport, I realized we had lost that twelve-inch 'space', so necessary to Americans. Everyone was my height and with the hundreds of people milling around, it was like we had stepped on a giant ant -hill. Jim's new Aide, Commander Skip Wright, a six-foot four man who had no trouble rising above it all, met us and I watched the two of them, head and shoulders above the crowd, cross the airport to the immigration office. They left me with their three briefcases and a bad case of building claustrophobia.

The trip to Taipei was a study in difficulties. From the Tokyo airport, in an official car with a Japanese driver, we drove the wrong way down a one-way street, sirens screaming, cheating death every foot of the way. A helicopter took us to the Atsugi Naval Air Facility where we spent a quick overnight. Then, on to Okinawa and the realization we would be heading directly into the path of a typhoon over Taiwan. Another overnight accompanied by much serious map study in the weather office and finally, because the Chinese had laid on an official welcoming ceremony on the airport runway, we took off in an Air force fighter jet straight into the teeth of the storm.

It was pouring rain when we touched down, but there they stood on the tarmac, waiting for us to descend and participate. With water running down my face and off my chin, I joined the Chinese dignitaries' wives, spoke my few words of "Glad to be here" Chinese" and stood in my little chalked circle. Jim stood in an open jeep and inspected the nearly drowned Chinese troops.

The wind was increasing with each moment. The ceremonies ended. We hurried through the terminal and into a waiting official car for a hair-raising trip up a mountain, dodging falling rocks and pieces of trees. At the bottom of a narrow gravel road that appeared to go straight up, I fell asleep. It was my only defense.

Jim wakened me to two armed guards on either side of the big iron gates to our Quarters. The guards looked familiar: At the airport, as we were landing, there were armed men in combat dress along the runway. Two questions came to mind: Was this martial law and what were we getting into?

Large trees were being uprooted all around us as the winds reached peak force. We ran for the tall, red lacquered doors of the Quarters A only to have them opened by a small, slight Chinese who smiled, giggled and nodded nonstop. He was Hogo, our houseboy and a welcome sight. We were soaked to the skin. There was no electricity because of the storm and the Quarters were almost empty of furniture. It would be six weeks before ours arrived.

An old Corgi dog with tongue lolling, was keeping close to Hogo and as my eyes adjusted to the dim light, I saw a man, spread eagle against large panes of glass on the porch, trying to put up metal shutters to protect the windows. He was on the outside, as wet as we were, and as he put up each sheet of metal, it flew off and sailed down the mountain. We beckoned him in, indicating it was a lost cause.

We met Michael Tatosian, a Master Chief Petty Officer on Jim's staff, past Seal, and extensive duty in Vietnam. He had held every dangerous job the Navy had to offer, and was the man who would help me whenever I needed anything. We all dried off with Quarters towels and sat on straight dining room chairs in the darkness. Jim sent Skip, his Aide, home to his family a mile up the mountain.

Just as Hogo found the candles, we heard a crash from the guest room. Jim's briefcases were in that room and we all ran for the door with Baron, the Corgi behind me as I followed the men into the room. Tiles from the neighbor's roof had ripped off and smashed the windows and a waterfall was pouring in, flooding the floor. As I grabbed the door frame, Baron fastened his teeth on my right heel and hung on. The wind caught the door and it was only my knocked over umbrella that prevented it from slamming on my hand. Keeping my cool with teeth in my heel and a full-fledged typhoon in our guest room was enough to make me yell for help.

Jim's only comment was, "I don't know why you get so clutched." It crossed my mind to pick up the umbrella and give him a whack.

Down one of the halls of the dark cavernous house, we found a bed and exhausted, wet and hungry, collapsed in our clothes for the night. Our luggage would come up the mountain the next day.

Morning dawned gray and yellow with the promise of more storms to come. With candles, and Baron behind me, I explored the expansive and quite beautiful house provided by the Chinese government, that would be our home for the next three years. Baron belonged to Jim's predecessor and was awaiting shipment back to the States. Knowing what was ahead for the old fellow, I forgave the heel incident and we became friends. However, I tried to keep my feet out from his line of sight.

As he ambled along beside me, we found the long, wide glass enclosed porch off the living room, and sure there must be a spectacular view, I saw only driving rain and fog. Actually, we were so high on the mountain, we were encased in clouds. My decorating instincts kicked in and I mentally placed our furniture in the many rooms. It would do very well.

Eventually, when they could brave the storm and get up the steep hill to the house, the Staff of five appeared. Hogo, who lived full time at the Quarters, was the keeper of the keys and gave the orders. He had served Taiwan Defense Commanders (TDC) for twenty-three years and though he spoke a broken pidgin English, understood every word we said. Mama San, round with an inscrutably pleasant smile on her face was the laundress, brass polisher and cook for the many guards that surrounded the house. Papa San, the gardener, beat the snakes out of the flower garden and tended the Olympic-sized swimming pool. A Phillipino cook who couldn't cook, lasted one week and was replaced -- by another Phillipino cook who was not much better and slept a lot – off and on the job.

Then there was Seargent Hsiu. A career Army man of some thirty years with a wife and family, he was my driver and protector. Trained in the martial arts, he could kill with his bare hands and he never let me out of his sight once we left the Quarters. He became my best friend.

When the typhoon moved down-island and the sky cleared, I saw for the first time, the view that would sustain me through the troubled times ahead. A dragon spine of high mountains to the left, marched south into the retreating clouds. In front and at the foot of the mountain we lived on was the very old and very wet village of Tien Mou. The rice paddies were flooded, as was the river that wound through them. More mountains to the right and perched on the highest was the Cultural College, a study in ancient beauty that took my breath away. With clouds at its base, it floated, and the tilted tiled roof corners, Chinese colors and simple grandeur completely captivated me. This was what I had always imagined China to be. But the time would come when I would learn the power of an angry mob of students it housed. The wet guards I now saw behind trees and bushes in our backyard would protect us against all threats, until *we* became the enemy.

Jim, of course, reported to his office immediately, despite falling trees and rolling rocks. Time, tide and a new command do not wait. The phones eventually worked and Skip called to tell me the Chinese government was allocating money to redecorate Quarters A. Imagine that! I could do anything I wanted to this gorgeous place and somebody else would foot the bill. It was almost as good as strolling down the Champs Elysees in Paris.

Under the moldy carpet, I found the mother lode -- inlaid teak floors. Somebody besides me would paint the walls, gray-green from mildew, and sheers on the windows would put us in the clouds. I made notes, searched my memory for ideas and called Skip with the first installment. Throughout the conversation, I heard a clicking sound and wondered if the typhoon had damaged the phone system.

Later, I would learn that our phones were tapped, our conversations recorded and every room in this magnificent ivory tower was bugged. This, and the armed guards surrounding the house, would take some getting used to.

The 'Ivory Tower' was not just a romantic description. It fit. Jim's Command was a joint one; Navy, Marine, Army and Air Force. There is a clear distinction between the branches of the military, although they work together. Among the wives, the rule was the same. I was high on a mountaintop in a spectacular house with acres of official functions to attend and therefore, untouchable. Although I was never made to feel unwelcome, there was little interest in who I was. The Wives Luncheons came and went, the cocktail parties flourished, but our schedule was rigid.

Five nights a week, we attended official Chinese dinners but he weekend was ours. The ladies who stood in the pounding rain at the airport were the same gracious hostesses at these dinners. They were the mandarin class of China, educated, world-wise and they became good friends. I must have amused them with my lack of knowledge of their culture, but their faces never gave them away. My own uncertainty was message enough.

Patricia Linder

CHAPTER THIRTY

During the renovation on Quarters A, we moved into the Hilton Hotel in downtown Taipei and I was sternly warned to remain in the hotel during Jim's hours away.

A doctor had been found for my eyes and Sgt. Hsiu in an official car, drove me to the Veteran's Hospital for my first appointment. We parked directly in front and, as I clutched my medical record, he marched me to an Otis elevator: 'Capacity: twenty-one', that today, held close to fifty people, waiting to go up. As the door closed, he must have noticed the panic on my face. One hour later, he was waiting for me at the bottom of the staircase as I chose to walk down the eight floors of steps rather than brave the elevator again.

Dr. Lin was the ophthalmologist to the Premier and because of Jim's position, was also mine. An older man, he spoke little English. Although he studied my records at length, I wondered if he understood any of it. His office was crowded with the newest machines, but I noticed many of them weren't plugged into the electric outlets. Could it be he didn't know how to use them? Or the directions were in English? Despite my unease, I liked Dr. Lin and as we saw each other on a monthly basis, came to respect his old -world knowledge. To him, I was a puzzle and a challenge; one that in time, would be treated with ancient Chinese philosophies.

We received our first dinner invitation during our stay at the Hilton. *'President and Mrs. Yen Chia-kan request the honor of your presence at dinner on.....'* Understandably, the heavy card that spelled the beginning of our official social life, intrigued me and I studied the guest list from Jim's briefcase with curiosity. Besides the President and Mrs. Yen, the American Ambassador and his wife, Len and Anne Unger, Chris and Helen Soong, (head of the Chinese Joint Chiefs of Staff), and the top Admiral of their Navy, David and Linda Tso. And us. Ten people, six of whom carried names I must learn, remember and pronounce correctly. I practiced. Ordering lunch from room service, I requested chop sticks and practiced some more. When the evening finally arrived, I slipped into a moderate V-necked gown and pronounced myself ready to enter the lion's den.

They were gracious, as they looked us over. Meals in China are almost always served at round tables, spouses across from each other and a revolving smaller table on top that holds the many dishes offered for the evening. The American Ambassador was on my right, the President on my left. The dinner proceeded with dignity and decorum In deference to their guests, English was spoken and I could easily follow the conversations. The questions directed to me always concerned our children, how many we had, their gender and ages.

I did pretty well until dessert. Having no trouble with the chopsticks and feeling like I had made points with my dexterity, I failed to notice everyone had switched to spoons for the small bowls of lichi nuts in syrup. Continuing with my chopsticks, I picked up one of the slippery things, lifted it to my mouth and realized it had fallen off and slipped down my V-necked dress. There was a general intake of breath, and when the Ambassador who had missed the whole thing, turned to ask if there was anything he could do to help me, I said, "Mr. Ambassador, this is something about which you can do nothing." Since the lichi nut wasn't going anywhere, I picked up my spoon and continued with dessert.

The party moved to a different plane. There was laughter, a less formal attitude and relief that I could laugh at myself, and wasn't too embarrassed to continue dinner. After dessert as liqueurs were served, I nodded to the one that sounded like the golden Italian Galliano. It was not. Taking my first sip, I realized someone had poured high- octane gasoline into my glass. I had nothing but fumes in my mouth. The expression on my face brought more laughter as I learned about Kaolien, the Chinese brandy.

All in all, it was a good party and with my unrehearsed disasters, the mood was one of relaxed friendship. Jim was understanding about it all, but I'm sure he wondered what was ahead for us if tonight was representative of our next three years. .

People began to take on identity to me, as did the island of Taiwan itself. Jim's Aide, Skip Wright, proved that all six feet four inches of him was there to be relied upon. Although he had been in Taiwan only a few short months before we arrived, he often had the answers to murky questions I couldn't work my way through. He was a genial man with an open face and a good sense of humor – a must in dealing with any Admiral's wife. His gentle advice was there before I could kick the wall in total frustration. Skip's wife, Shannon was a tall, serene woman with a cloud of dark hair and a warm, lazy smile. They had two small, towheaded children. It was a nice family. I was glad they lived nearby.

When Skip called to say the ship carrying our furniture and car had finally arrived in Keelung, the harbor north of Taipei, I felt all the old instincts of nesting. The Quarters were finished and waiting, I had a book full of notes and was ready for the movers to offload. Mike Tatosian came to help, his compact body wound like a spring. On alert, he watched each piece as it came through the door. As my cherrywood kneehole desk was brought into the house in three pieces, Mike hurried to my side.

"Now don't worry, Mrs. Linder. I know a man in Taipei who can put that back together and refinish it so you'll never know anything ever happened to it."

After so many moves with so much damage to our furniture, I thought I was immune to feelings of loss, but the desk was important and, swallowing my tears, I put its fate into Mike's hands. He didn't disappoint me. The marred, scratched and gouged pieces were duly noted and he made arrangements to have them taken to downtown Taipei for repair. Eventually, they were returned in better condition than when we had purchased them.

Sgt. Hsiu at the wheel, our car rolled majestically into the driveway. The good Sergeant looked like he was heaven-bound, as well he should. Just before we left Norfolk to come to Taipei, 'they' suggested Jim buy a new car befitting his position in Taiwan. We had purchased a new one two months earlier and he found himself faced with replacing it with a brand new Cadillac Seville. Silver, no less. I had no idea how much it cost or how much money we lost on the transaction, but I filed it under 'hidden benefits'. Whatever the loss, the look on Sgt. Hsiu's face was worth every penny. He immediately drove it down to the lower level of the Quarters where the kitchens and garages were located, and lovingly washed and polished it inside and out. I had never seen the car. Jim purchased it in Norfolk and made the arrangements for it to go directly onto the ship carrying our household goods. Watching the pretty thing slide past the front windows, I knew it would be fun to sit in the back with the Sergeant as my chauffeur and feel posh. The license plate read *'001'*. I could live with that.

The house was a jumble, as it always is until, through painstaking sorting and stashing, things find their place and the jumble becomes a home. I didn't mind too much. The Quarters were large enough to hold all we had, with the promise that some shopping would have to be done to fill it up. Never mind, the exotic pieces would go home with us and Taiwan would be a part of the Linder family for many years to come.

Jim and I working over the weekend and on Sunday afternoon, finally agreed we both needed a walk. Strolling down the circular driveway, through the iron gates and on up the narrow dirt road that climbed past our neighbors' homes, we admired the view, talked about the move and the next week's schedule.

Out of the corner of my eye, I noticed a man in khaki behind us, carrying a brown paper sack. Each time we slowed, he slowed. Each time we stopped, he stopped.

"Jim, somebody's following us. I've been watching and he's timed to us. It looks like he's carrying his lunch. Should we stop so he can eat?"

"No. We keep going. That's not his lunch -- that's a gun. He's our bodyguard."

Oh grand.

I began to appreciate my free-wheeling days around Europe where nobody found it necessary to monitor my every move. Even the loneliness was not as bad as I had thought. At least I had learned how to deal with that. This was a different matter. I began to feel claustrophobic again.

"Dear, could we talk about this a little bit, or am I supposed to guess at why there's a man with the gun following us and armed guards all over Quarters A? While we're at it, could you give me a little direction on telephone taps and bugs in the ceiling fans in every room?"

"I guess if we'd had briefings before we left the States, they would have explained this sort of thing." He looked decidedly uncomfortable with my questions.

"Oh yes, briefings. Nobody ever explained why we never received any."

This was great. I could fling all sorts of chestnuts in the fire and maybe get some answers.

"Don't know. It seemed strange to me at the time, but the Department of State goes by its own rules and being a member of the military, I don't always understand their logic."

His face indicated he would like the conversation to switch to something bland like the weather. It wasn't the first time I felt there were more things afoot than what we were led to believe. But it was still a feeling and until Jim chose to enlighten me about Taiwan politics, I could only sidestep the issue.

Patricia Linder

CHAPTER THIRTY ONE

The house was straight, there was money in my pocket and Sergeant Hsiu was at the wheel of '*001*'. I was going shopping. Downtown Taipei was still a mystery to me, having seen it only at night as we sped to another dinner party. Today, I would jump-start the Chinese economy.

Even with all of our own furniture, the Quarters were so large, there were empty spots that needed filling; another living room set, porch furniture and pieces for the large sitting room in our bedroom wing. There was no allocated money for this. We either made do or paid for it ourselves. Jim added to my furniture stash and I was ready to take on the shopkeepers of Taipei.

Smooth driver as he was, the car and its license plate parted the way and, feeling a little like Moses and the Red Sea, we sped down Yangmingshan, the mountain we lived on. The typhoon damage had been removed and with Nature at her most forgiving, one would never know of the terrible devastation just a few short weeks ago. It was a day of sunshine, flowers, green trees and hordes of people. This island was roughly the size of Florida with only one third of it, livable because of its high mountains, and that one third supported a population count of over twenty-two million souls.

A good many of them drove cars or motorcycles that were either directly in front of or cozying up on either side of our car. I wanted to ask Sgt. Hsiu to throttle back a little so I could see what was flashing by, but he was intent on his driving.

As we left an intersection, I noticed a bus, belching black smoke, coming toward us. Suddenly, a motorcycle flashed around it and, cutting in too quickly, was hit by the bus. A body flew through the air and landed just in front of us near the curb on our side of the road. It looked like a crumpled heap of clothing, with nothing where it should have been.

We drove straight on.

"Sgt. Hsiu, we must stop and help. That man may be dying."

"No Missy."

"Sgt. Hsiu, we can't just leave him. We have to do something."

"No Missy."

We were speeding down the mountain and once I realized there would be no help from us, I subsided, intent on framing my explanation to the Sergeant why we should have stopped. At the foot of the mountain, he pulled into the TDC Compound where Jim's office was, stopped the car and, looking straight ahead, said quietly, "Missy, it is not safe to stop. People see this car and know you are in it. I must keep you safe. That is my job."

I couldn't think of a thing to say and simply leaned forward and placed my hand on his shoulder. He nodded and we pulled out onto Chungsan North Road to find the first item on my list.

There was underground terrorism on this island. I knew that. Letter bombs were commonplac. The governor had been injured by one the week we arrived, and I wondered just how widespread the danger was. It was a hotbed of political unrest and if I was in jeopardy sitting in my own car, where was I safe? This was shaping up to be a very restrictive tour of duty.

I was too shaken by the accident to concentrate on something as frivolous as wicker for the porch. But the good Sergeant, in his wisdom, took me to a tiny store that held only beautiful things and where I saw the treasures of China; jades of every color, fragile, tissue-thin porcelains with scenes from the mountains and lakes of the many mainland provinces, carved ivories in incredible shapes. My eyes feasted as I held a carved piece of lavender jade in my hand. Cold to the touch, it drew warmth from my skin as though it belonged there. And the shock lessened.

"Thank you, Sgt. Hsiu. You've given me a perfect hour here and I feel better for it." He nodded and I saw a faint smile. "We can go on for a while, but I'll want to go home soon. We'll come down another time." Again, his nod and he returned to the car parked directly in front of the shop, opened the door and saw me safely inside. Only then did I notice that no one had been allowed in the store while I was there. As we left, customers began filtering in.

Later, on the way up Yangmingshan Mountain, we passed the scene of the accident and all that remained of a young man was his pair of shoes. They sat by the curb, waiting for his family to come take them. The shoes would tell them he was dead. Would I ever understand this country and its people?

Jim's command was closely aligned to the Chinese military command on the island. The United States supplied weapons and training for the troops. They trained all the time with a determination that spoke of either returning to and taking back the mainland that held their ancestors, or defending Taiwan against communist invaders. It was serious business, this art of survival for a place of such vulnerability, but they had centuries of practice behind them and as focused as they were, would give any enemy pause before confronting them.

We toured the bases near Taipei, their Parliament, the military installations on other parts of the island and their harbors. A plane came with the job and we fondly referred to it as the Blue Goose. The thirty-five year old DC 3 sat on the runway, nose pointed to the heavens and its bottom firmly planted on the tarmac. As we touched down on yet another unfamiliar location, the complexities of this island were like a Chinese puzzle.

Mid-island was a tribe of aborigines. On our visit there, with Jim in full uniform, a circle was formed and with each of us holding a baby, we moved to a tribal dance. It was a communal village with the children belonging to one and all and they charmed us.

In Kaoshung, the industrial city on the southern tip of Taiwan, we inspected steel mills and the shipbuilding yards. The oil tankers of the world were built there. One would have to see them to believe them. They stretched for city blocks.

Kaoshung had refinery cracking plants and cement factories. In the hotel at night, I cleaned the packed cement dust out of my eyes and prayed for an early return to Taipei. At an official luncheon before we boarded the Blue Goose, I ate what a Chinese General across the table assured me was "slake soup, hen hau." Assuming it was a type of fish and knowing 'hen hau' meant 'very good', I finished it off, only to find I had smacked my lips over a bowl of 'snake soup'.

I came to realize that by seeing nearly all of Taiwan, I was also seeing China, itself. The island was a microcosm of the many provinces of China, its people and its topography were as varied. At a stop sign one day, I looked at the crowd waiting to cross and my eyes met those of a tall man, a Mongolian and another Ghengis Khan. For just a moment, I was on the steppes of Asia. Each face belonged to a certain place in the sprawling giant of China and the longer we stayed, the easier it became to identify the differences.

The day dawned silent, nothing moved. The sky carried a faint shade of yellow green that would deepen as the hours wore on. In Iowa, it would be prelude to a tornado, but here, I wondered if another typhoon was building in the China Seas.

We were deep in sleep when the bed rose up off the floor and danced across the room. The sound was primordial – a grinding that told us the earth was shifting position. Earthquake. There was nothing we could do but hang on and in the eerie silence that followed, we heard the first slap of raindrops on the windowpanes. The rain would last for days with floods that claimed scores of lives. Many TDC families lived on a nearby mountain and the earthquake, followed by the torrential flood heavily damaged their homes.

I answered the ringing phone to hear the frantic voice of one of the TDC wives at the other end.

"Pat, this is Kay. We're in trouble up on our mountain."

"What's happening, Kay? Is it the earthquake or the rain?"

"Both, really. There is some structural damage to our homes, but the water is pouring down the mountainside and that's our worst concern. Our doors are sprung so the it's coming through our houses."

"Good heavens, Kay – are you all right? Have you been able to move your furniture out of the way?"

"Yes, we're okay. We've been doing a lot of stacking with our best things on the top. My neighbor, Mary Anne, has her mother visiting from the States and when the water broke through their back door, it carried the chair she was sitting in right out the front door."

"Kay, how awful. Was she injured at all?"

"No, but I think she wants to go home."

I had to smile. This was one story that would last a long time once she was back in her own neighborhood.

Kay sounded concerned. "Are you all right at Quarters A?"

"We are. The house held through the earthquake and hopefully, we won't slide down the mountain into Tien Mou on the flood - waters. Kay, is there anything we can do to help?"

"Our husbands are home, so that's about all any of us can do. I really called to tell you a baby is missing. She went out with the rush of water and most of the men are searching for her now."

Damn. A baby.

Kay gave the name of the parents and I promised to pass the word on to Jim as soon as we hung up. I didn't know the family, but could imagine the terror they must feel, not knowing where their child was.

The search lasted all night and her tiny body was found at the base of the mountain the next day. It was a time of mourning for all of the Defense Command.

At the bottom of that same mountain was the English-speaking American school. The raging waters nearly wiped it out. The American Ambassador called and we all arranged to meet at the school when the rain stopped to help with the big job of cleaning up the devastation. With mops and buckets, scrub brushes and bottles of bleach, we righted the desks and chairs, then scrubbed the slimy residue left by the flood. The men and women of TDC came, despite the condition of their own homes. It was more important to get the children back in school and on schedule. By some miracle, there were only minor injuries and within the week, life resumed its placid, tropical pace.

Hogo our houseboy, had tested me when we first arrived. He was a friendly little man who ran the Quarters smoothly. Always impeccable in his black pants and white open-collared shirt, he knew every inch of the house, what it needed and, as time went by, what we needed to live in it comfortably. When the evening came for our first dinner party, I asked Hogo and Mama San to come to the dining room. I had set up a place setting, complete with china, flatware and crystal. The two of them stood on the opposite side of the table and watched as I explained this was the way every place should look. Thirty guests were expected. Many nods, many smiles and a giggle or two, and I headed for the shower. Twenty minutes before the doorbell rang, I checked the dining room and knew I had been challenged. Each place setting was exactly opposite what I had shown them. Hogo had been setting American tables for twenty-three years and I guessed this was his way of finding out who was boss.

"Hogo, there's something not right about our table tonight. Do you see it, too?"

"No, Missy." Giggle, giggle.

"It's backwards, Hogo. Everything must be reversed. According to my watch, we have just fifteen minutes to do it. Better get Mama San."

I fixed one place correctly, then drifted off to check for ashtrays and matches. In ten minutes, the table was correct. He had tested and apparently, I had passed. There were no more glitches of his doing.

The one disaster of the evening came with dessert. Having walked the sleepy Phillipino cook 'Naldo, through the preparation of Baked Alaska, I set the bottle of Couvousier on the pantry counter, explaining about the pouring and lighting of the French brandy. I should have checked if he was fully awake. He was to light the Baked Alaska, then bring it through the swinging pantry door, presenting it to the guests in all its flaming glory.

Dinner went well. Things were warm instead of hot, but no one seemed to mind. As we waited for dessert, 'Naldo hit the pantry door with his rump, lighting the mound of meringue as he turned to enter the dining room. But 'Naldo had finished off the Couvousier himself and substituted Kaolien brandy instead. When the flame touched the liquid, it exploded. Fascinated guests watched ice cream, meringue and yellow sponge cake slide down the walls of the dining room. A bleary-eyed 'Naldo hiccuped once and fled.

"Shall we move to the living room for coffee and check ourselves for meringue?'

Shocked silence turned into gales of laughter over the floor- show we provided and I would be no threat to the perfect hostesses on this island. It was a good party.

Patricia Linder

CHAPTER THIRTY TWO

The MAYDAY! MAYDAY! call echoed through the cabin of the Blue Goose as we flew over the South China Sea on our way to the Phillipines. Due south of Taiwan, and visible on a clear day, the hundreds of islands that make up that chain, lay ahead in the misty morning. A ship was in trouble, sending the universal signal to anyone in the area. Our plane circled, each of us at a window, but the ocean lay empty. The pilot passed along the information and voiced his concern about the amount of gas that the Blue Goose was using to search. Reluctantly, the decision was made to continue on our way. Jim had business at Subic Bay on the west coast of Luzon and I was dropped off in the middle of the island at Clark Air Force Base for my appointment with an American ophthalmologist.   Arrangements were made for me to catch a ride in a marine helicopter and join him in Subic Bay, down -island two days later.

My eyes were dimming out and I began to notice a tentative quality to my active life as my sight diminished. Nobody wants to walk into a wall, but unless someone came up with an answer, I was headed in that direction. As always, everyone in the Eye Clinic had to take a look. I suppose as diseases go, mine was a rare one and the damage it was causing on a continuing basis was interesting to a doctor, but devastating to me. I was too young and there was too much to do to give in to its restrictions.

On the morning of my flight to Subic, I was hustled into the yawning hatch of the biggest helicopter I had ever seen. The weather had turned foul and a full-fledged storm was moving in. One other passenger came aboard and after dutifully donning the big Micky Mouse ear protectors, we settled into the bucket seats that lined the wall. With pencil and paper, he introduced himself as an Air Force colonel on his way to Subic. I did the same. It was a terrifying ride, as the helo dipped and soared, rocked and bumped its way through the storm. Below us was a sea of jungle so dense, I realized if we went down, no one would ever find the plane. Or us. But the pilot knew what he was doing and we gently set down on a sunny runway in Subic Bay.

This trip around the South Pacific would also include the island of Kinmen, or Quemoy, before the Generalissimo renamed it. Tucked up under the bulging belly of China's east coast, this small piece of land sustained artillery fire from Mainland China only 400 yards across the water. The Chinese communists fired on Kinmen on even days and Kinmen fired back on odd days. Then, the people of Kinmen took the shell casings and pounded them into the prized chefs' knives and cleavers that are marketed world-wide.

We helped launch a propaganda balloon that would catch the prevailing wind and sail into Communist China. It carried toothpaste, toothbrushes, children's clothing and the message of how much better it was to live in a free world. Happily, I cut the tether hoping some family would get the message.

Jim's distraction grew. Although he was home every night, our schedule over the past months and the bugs in the fan left us little time to communicate. I had been instructed not to discuss anything about Taiwan in the official car on our way to anywhere. His driver understood English and I had no trouble following orders there.

I did not like Sgt Fan. I was afraid of him.

So here we were, Shore Duty and no chance to talk. Because we were followed when we went anywhere in the Seville, Jim purchased a small, second-hand car and leaving early one Sunday morning, before the motorcycle brigade could get into place, we drove over the mountains to the west coast of Taiwan. With us was Suzy Wong, a six-month old toy Japanese Spitz puppy Sergeant Hsiu and I had rescued from a watery ditch where someone had dumped the litter.. A few months before, realizing I was lonesome, I posted a notice on the Commissary bulletin board that I was looking for a little, white dog. A few days later, one of the TDC wives called about some puppies in the ditch near her home, and Sgt Hsiu and I hurried to the street not far from the Quarters. We gathered up the one surviving puppy that had climbed out and was wobbling toward '001', wrapped her in a towel, and she rode home in style. We named her Suzie Wong. She was a survivor.

Today, as we sped toward the west, there were no motorcycles behind us, only Suzie who was in a state of hysteria over being included on our trip to the beach. With Mama San's cooking and the loving care of everybody at the Quarters, she had grown into a silky-haired enchantress with almond eyes and a perpetual grin.

I was anxious to see the beach and breathe air clear of the pollution of Taipei. But the beach was coated with oil from a tanker wreck southwest of the island. The prevailing currents had washed the gummy, sticky stuff onto the wide, white strip of sand. The smell was industrial.

Sitting on a clean rock with Suzie in my lap, I asked Jim if he could tell me more about his job and what he did.

"I haven't wanted to discuss it at the Quarters because it's not just for anybody to hear."

"I understand that and you know I'll keep what you say to myself, but I can't help being curious. When you went to Kaoshung, last week, what did you do?"

"We visited the Chinese Marine Headquarters and had briefings on their readiness and materiel requirements. Then we witnessed a parade, celebrating their anniversary."

This was nothing but more Navy memo talk.

"How do they compare with our Marines?"

"They were proud and well-informed about modern warfare tactics. Young as they are, they seemed pretty dedicated. We visited the Naval Base and their Naval Academy facilities. They have a small number of diesel submarines that were predominantly used as training ships, and we were briefed on the tactical use of subs in this area."

He was being very careful.

"You're talking about the Taiwan Straits and the threat from China?"

"Right, but these ships were not capable of conducting combat operations."

"But with their shipyards, can't they build submarines that are combat ready?

"They don't need to. They can obtain current submarine technology through other sources more economically."

Of course. Countries had been buying or leasing older ships from the U.S. for a long time. I recalled seeing them in Spain and Greece.

I asked questions about the TDC and Embassy personnel. It was important to know something about the other Americans, to be aware of the undercurrents that are always part of a command. But I stayed away from Jim's change of attitude about his job. Another time. This was the only day we had to relax. Jeff's graduation was the last of May and I assumed it would extend into June with time for the family and a trip to Bethesda Naval Hospital. I knew Jim would be scheduled for briefings in Washington and we talked over our plans.

The past months had been hectic ones filled with trips, official dinners, a spectacular Christmas with gifts rolling in and the wildly colorful Chinese New Year. TDC hosted a holiday party at the Officers' Club that included a visit from the Premier of the Republic of China. Aside from my mistaking his Aide with his medals and gold braid for the Premier (bad night for my eyes), it was quite successful. We liked the Chinese people and they liked us.

But I missed the children more than I imagined possible. We had almost always had Christmas with one or both, but now, they could have been on another planet. Although we corresponded regularly, I was missing the growing up of our granddaughters – times that could never be recaptured. The month of May couldn't come quickly enough.   Jeff and his college graduation crept into my thoughts on a daily basis and I made lists of plans for our short time in the States.

The political climate of Taipei had an edgy feel to it. This was the year of the Taiwan Defense Treaty renewal between the ROC and the U.S.. Once again, the term *'handwriting on the wall'* was heard more often.   President Jimmy Carter was looking for a legacy and normalizing with China would be a dandy.   President Nixon, a Republican, had already made overtures by going to China and toasting everybody including Confucious, so why not finish the job? Obviously, Taiwan was nervous about this whole scenario.

Having worked for Congress, my interest was piqued. Running up my antennae, I listened carefully to all conversations and began to fill in the pieces. We moved in the upper echelon of government and despite the carefully choreographed conversations, body language told me a lot.

But I personally had 'no need to know' and once again, fell into the sinkhole of a security risk. That's where Navy wives often found themselves and supposing it was an offshoot of one of World War II's better slogans, 'Loose lips sink ships', I bided my time, gathered my own intelligence and drew private conclusions that were disquieting at least.

Jim was late on this Thursday evening. There was no party scheduled and I was looking forward to a night at home with maybe some poolside conversation. We knew that once Hogo had made sure we needed nothing more, he would retire to his room next to the kitchen and aside from the ubiquitous guards positioned behind trees and bushes, we were alone. Suzie curled up contentedly between our chairs.

"Jim, I've been tweaking my lists for our trip back to the States in May. Jeff seemed a little vague about his graduation date, but we know approximately when we'll need to be there."

Jim nodded and looked at the mountains.

"I can go over the schedule as it is now, if you like."

Jim continued to look at the mountains.

"Dear, when last I heard, those mountains are stationary, in case you're waiting for them to move." I began to feel uneasy.

"We will have to miss Jeff's graduation." He spoke softly, but his voice had the unyielding quality I knew so well.

His jaw was set, the straight line of his dark brows was down and his full lips had thinned. His eyes, always the foreteller of his moods, were narrowed and I felt like the enemy.

"Please tell me you're not serious."

"There's been heavy message traffic this week and I am required to be in Washington in mid-July."

I was waiting for him to face me squarely and tell me the reasons why. The mountains had his undivided attention.

"Jim, I don't usually say things like this, but what you've told me is unacceptable. I will not allow it to happen." I steeled myself to say something I really didn't want to. "All my married life, you and the Navy have told me what I can and cannot do, usually at the expense of our marriage and our children. I have no intention of giving chapter and verse on the inequities we've put up with, but you cannot tell me I must miss our son's graduation from college."

He looked at me and there was anger in his face. "I will do what I have to do. We can't afford two trips back and my orders are to be in Washington in July." I was left with his profile as he resumed his study of the mountains.

"Then I will go without you." It had happened in the past and it could happen again.

"You can't make the trip alone and you know it. Besides, your presence will be needed here." His face could have been cut from marble. I began to think his heart was.

I could feel anger and helplessness welling up. Suzie, sensing something was wrong, laid her head on my knee and looked at me as I burst into tears. *These damned eyes – when I need you, you aren't there for me.* Oblivious of the guards and Hogo lurking in the kitchen doorway, I ran up the stairs to the bedroom with Suzie on my heels, flung myself on the bed, covered my head with a pillow and cried it out.

Later, I paced the room, going over possible scenarios in my mind but always coming back to the realities of my life.

"Dammit" I knew I was beaten and once again, would do what the Navy and my husband told me to. I tried to imagine why Jim was so unreasonable and assumed Taiwan's future had something to do with it.

"Taiwan's future can go to blazes. My son's graduation is the beginning of *his* future and my future is to share it with him."

I was oblivious of the listening device in the fan. They could make of it whatever they wanted to. I thought of Jim's graduation from the Naval Academy with both sets of parents attending and all the festivities we shared, but comparisons are deadly and I wearily pushed them from my mind.

Mutually, we knew this had to be talked out and on Sunday morning early, we escaped in our little car, found a deserted side road and faced each other.

"Am I to be given any explanation about your decision, or is this another 'no need to know'?"

"I'm afraid that's what it is."

"Take it or leave it – those are my choices?"

"I'm sorry, Patti, but it has to be that way, at least for now. I'm just as frustrated as you are, knowing I will miss Jeff's graduation."

I wasn't hearing him. "I'm asking for a logical and truthful explanation of why our son will graduate from college with none of his family present."

"When I am ordered to do something, I do it, no questions asked."

My response was swift. "And no quarter given. Jim, however you choose to do it, by telephone or letter, the message *will* come from you. I have never spoken against you to the children, but my only request is that you tell him in such a way, he will have a minimum of hurt. And if you can get him to understand, maybe someday, he can explain it to me."

End of conversation.

My eyes went haywire, as they always did with stress.   Dr. Lin got right to the point.

"Linder Tai Tai, I want to put you in the hospital and give you typhoid fever."

Dear God. The whole male world had it in for me.

"Dr. Lin, why would you want to do that?   I've had shots to keep from *having* typhoid fever."

"I think maybe high fever kill inflammation in eyes."

"But with that kind of fever, I could have brain or heart damage."

"Meyogwanchi."   That's the Chinese word for 'never mind'.

I slid out of the chair, shook his hand and said, "Dr. Lin, don't call me, I'll call you."

Jeff's graduation day came and went. There was no conversation about it, as there was little conversation about anything. We lived the life, fulfilled our requirements and made ready to leave for Jim's briefings in Washington in July. Our visits with the children and parents would come at the end of our stay in the U.S..

Bethesda Hospital hooked me up to the machines, shook their collective heads and passed me on to the National Institute of Health, which did the same. I would simply have to live with the knowledge of blindness, the only variable being -- when. But there wasn't time to dwell on it, so I put it out of my mind and instead, thought about our coming reunions with the children. I never asked Jim what he said to our son, but when we arrived in Austin, Jeff assured me there was no problem about our missing his graduation.

"Mom, I had to work every day that week and would not have made it anyway. Besides, they don't hand you your sheepskin – they mail it to you. Too many graduating to do it any other way."

My God, how I loved this boy.

We touched down for our visit with Jamey, Bob and their two little ones, exclaimed how they had grown, did the Zoo and anything else we could think of to catch up and be the grandparents they deserved. Our visit with my mother and Jim's father had been fleeting, but I felt like I was good for another year.

Jim was more preoccupied than ever after his Washington briefings and I could feel the buildup of anger that never seemed to go away. We were on better terms after the family visit and I could only hope that someday, he would allow me into his life enough to help him through whatever was ahead.

When we entered Quarters A through its great red lacquered front doors, Suzie took a running leap and glued herself to the front of me. Hogo giggled non-stop and 'Naldo the cook, woke up long enough to welcome us back, then ambled back to the kitchen for his next nap. We gathered our messages and in answering them the next day, I found an acquaintance had invited me to tea. Not too unusual, but when I responded, she gave me the news that her husband was being posted to Hong Kong and she wished to see me one more time before they left.

Apparently my reputation for little white dogs had circulated, because the 'tea' was an excuse to give me Boom Boom, her pearly

301

white Chinese Pekinese and her maid, Julie. Holding a tea cup and the dog at the same time gave me little chance to say anything but 'yes' and although I had to pass on her maid, Boom Boom became a part of our family. Suzie thought she was a toy and within an hour, they were inseparable. We called them 'The Girls'. When Jim came home from the office, they waited for him inside the doors, then followed him down the hallway to the sitting room, their little white rumps switching.

My sixth sense about my husband prompted me to ask for a Sunday by ourselves. In the little car, we drove to Keelung, the port north of Taipei. Parking on a city street, we remained in the car and I wasted no time.

"What's bothering you, Jim?"

He was a man of few words and I knew I would only hear what I should hear – which was probably not much. But he needed to share what he could with someone.

"I'm disturbed about the level of protection of Taiwan. I know they have *us*, but we will probably go away someday and I don't know what will happen to them when that time comes. To try to explain this, I'll have to go back to the war in Vietnam."

The one thing I never wanted to do was go back to Vietnam, even in my thoughts.

"The Chinese Communists and Russia were supplying the Viet Cong with weapons and ordnance – most of it pretty sophisticated stuff. China's interest was, I suppose, territorial – the more countries they could add to their list of colonies, the stronger they would be."

"So that makes three Communist countries in league with each other?"

"That makes a lot of troops, many weapons and ordnance and when the war ended and we pulled out, we gave them the wherewithal to use what we left behind. And we left a lot."

"Are you getting around to telling me that China has all of that and could use it against Taiwan?"

"Why not? I'm sure it was divvied up among the three countries and along with the physical elements of war, was the technology that made it all work."

I was horrified. Our own weapons of war could be used against this tiny island. Not too unlike the scrap metal we sent to Japan to be used against us in World War II.

"Won't we always be there for them?"

"According to what I hear in the weekly Team meetings at the Embassy, we should all be paying closer attention to what's going on back home. There are some pretty serious economic problems and under the Carter Administration, the interest rates are going off the charts."

He continued. "Our foreign policy is directly tied to our own economy and that has to be our first priority. The military's primary objective here is protection against the enemy – and on a proximity basis, that would be China. State sees it as a diplomatic problem, one that can be solved by talking. You know how I feel about that."

Indeed I did. A dichotomy would always exist between the two. So often in the past, the 'talking' had lured us into convoluted situations that could only be resolved by the use of force, leaving the military as the bad guys.

"But Jim, there has to be both or the world would have destroyed itself centuries ago."

"I agree, but we're in a push-pull situation now with Taiwan. We're their umbrella of protection, but the question is, will our own economic problems override that?"

"What happens if we're not there for them?" I could guess the answer.

"The supposition is immediate invasion by the Chinese Communists, but that's based on Taiwan opinion. Nobody really knows until it happens."

On a hill high above our heads, I saw an immense statue of the Kuan Yin, Goddess of Compassion, and since it overlooked the ships in the water, Goddess of Protection. Her face was peaceful, benign as it is always presented. She towered above the whole city. I thought to myself, Lady, you have your work cut out for you.

CHAPTER THIRTY THREE

December *15, 1978*

The Chamber of Commerce was hosting its annual Christmas dinner dance. The Officers' Club looked festive and the band was good. We shared a table with the Ambassador and his wife, Ann, enjoyed a good dinner, listened to the usual round of speeches, then joined the other couples when the music began.

As Jim asked Ann to dance, Len and I rose to move onto the floor. Tlhis career diplomat was a handsome man in his impeccable tuxedo and a good dancer. His ability to make anyone feel comfortable, came from years of practice. Making small talk, I noticed a Marine in uniform heading in our direction.

"Len, there's a Marine coming our way and I'm pretty sure he wants to talk to you." I could feel the Ambassador stiffen.

Len turned his head quickly. The Marine stopped behind the Ambassador and spoke briefly into his ear, then waited for Len to follow him.

"Pat, forgive me, but we must return to the table. I have to find Jim. Tell Ann I'll have the official car drive her back to the Embassy." Signaling Jim to accompany them, the three men quickly left the ballroom. Realizing something had happened, Ann and I returned to the table to wait for instructions. I envied her calm presence of mind and knew it came from years of this sort of emergencies.

My confusion must have shown on my face, for she laid a hand over mine and said, "They'll be all right. Len has had a lot of practice at this."

A lot of practice at what?

Eventually, we were handed into our official cars and returned to our homes. I would not see my husband until late the next day.

Someone in the State Department in Washington, D.C, had sent a message to the Ambassador that the United States was breaking off diplomatic relations with the Republic of China.

The Taiwan Defense Treaty would not be renewed.

Diplomatic relations would be established with Communist China, instead. President Carter had found his legacy. The Ambassador had to waken the aging and infirm Premier in the early morning hours and deliver the bad news.

I was not to know this until the next morning at the TDC Compound. It was my turn to spend the day in the little boutique we maintained for the purpose of raising money for Chinese charities. With still no word from Jim, I opened up the shop and turned on the radio. As the other wives filtered in to begin the day's sales, the announcement was made about Taiwan and the United States. No one moved. I could see the dawning of understanding on their faces, then the beginning of fear.

"Pat, what does it mean? Are we in danger? Do you know what will happen next? Should we go home?'

The questions came thick and fast and not having any more information than anyone else, I could only tell them of the incident during last night's dance. But I would keep what Jim had previously shared with me in the back of my mind until the right time. I advised the girls to go home immediately, round up their children, then wait for word from their husbands in TDC.

Sgt. Hsiu had yet to hear the announcement. His eyebrows lifted a fraction when I asked him to help me close up the shop we had just opened, but he said nothing. Little Jimmy Chen who had for fifteen years, swept the floor and dusted the items for sale, looked suspicious and frightened. I tried to make him understand that we had to close because of something that had happened. Facing two inscrutable Chinese men, I knew I was out of my element because of language.

I took Jimmy's hand, looked him directly in his eyes and said, "You will be all right, Jimmy. You will know soon, but you will be all right. Don't be afraid." I knew this was his only source of income and I was the one who was afraid.

As Sgt. Hsiu handed me into the car, I said, "We'll talk on the way to the Quarters." Our eyes met before his brief nod and mine filled with tears at what I must say to this loyal man.

On the way up the mountain, I told him in simple terms about the radio announcement. His head turned toward me for just an instant and I could see he understood and did not blame me. I could not look the Chinese in the face as they peered into the car at each stoplight.

For the first time in my life, I was ashamed of my country.

At the Quarters, I found Mama San watching television in her little room off the kitchen. She knew. Her round face lifted to look at me and without hesitation I knelt beside her. She pulled my head in her ample lap and through my tears I apologized. She smoothed my hair and murmured her understanding.

"Meyogwanchi," she said. Never mind. .

Thus, our time of travail began. Jim returned to tell me what had happened and where we stood now. American children were pulled out of school and kept at home.

A general quarantine went into effect for all TDC families. Keeping off the streets for safety's sake, it was as though we had never existed. We were as unprotected now as were the people of Taiwan. There would be anger and hatred toward all American personnel connected to TDC. Overnight, we had become the enemy. I knew there were dark days ahead and they could only be faced one at a time.

All social life stopped. The holiday parties were canceled and the mound of gifts for our Chinese counterparts remained in the guestroom, wrapped and waiting. I felt suspended in time. No calls came from our Chinese friends and the ones from the TDC wives had a decidedly frantic quality to them. Their high school seniors would lose the entire year and many had already paid entrance fees to the colleges of their choice. Their husbands' career patterns were destroyed. The American wives who held jobs in the Compound or in Taipei, lost them. The list went on.

But the day Jim told me we had to speak together to the men and their families in the auditorium was one of the worst.

With his chin resting on a clenched hand, he said, "I have to tell them what's ahead in the way of evacuation procedures. There are very few moving companies under government contract and it's going to be tough, moving a couple of thousand people out in a hurry."

"How long do we have?"

"We'll know that when they send in the team from State to break the Treaty, but probably no more than two or three months and to do that, some will have to leave immediately. But I have to ask you to help me with something else. Will you tell them they can't take their pets back to the States? They will either have them put to sleep or find homes for them."

He was looking at the mountains again. "The few animals that have already been shipped back never made it. We can't take ours if nobody else can. We'll have to find homes for them. I know it will be hard to tell everyone, but I think you can soften the blow."

"I can't do it." I could feel the cracks in my dam beginning again.

"Yes, you can. We have to." No questions asked, no quarter given. Again.

It was penance for everything wrong I've ever done. Many in the audience of dependents knew I had two little dogs and the rules were the same for all of us. As Jim delivered blow after blow to these frightened, confused people, I knew he was as torn up inside as I was.

The riots began. Between the fifteenth of December and Christmas, the Chinese let us know how they felt. A sound truck parked in front of our Quarters, playing, at top volume for twenty-four hours, Aulde Lang Syne. I sent the Staff home and locked the doors.

The phones were ringing incessantly, but I was met with only silence when I said, hello. Afraid to take them off their hooks because of the possibility Jim might try to reach me, there was nothing left to do but wait it out with The Girls. The usually friendly and respectful guards were no longer anything but menacing. Their weapons were now pointed in the direction of the house.

Jim was at the Embassy for meetings, but the University students rioted and climbed the walls of that Compound. Because of a recent order from the Department of Defense, the Marine guards held empty guns. No ammunition was allowed, leaving the people inside without protection of any kind. The American flag was pulled down. What I didn't know was that the mob had been given orders to threaten but they could not kill.

Fists pounded on Quarters A's great red lacquered doors. The guards at the gate had let the Cultural College students onto the grounds. Rocks were thrown, but this house belonged to the Chinese government and they were under orders not to damage it.

Being built of stone, they concentrated their attacks on its walls. Making sure once more that every door was locked, I took The Girls to the sitting room, turned on the television to drown out the noise of the rioting mob and the ringing phones and held on.

At last, I called Skip at home where Jim had sent him to be with his family. Their house was only one short block from the College. I told him it was time for me to get out of the Quarters if I could. Surrounded as we were by hostile Chinese and with no idea if Jim was safe, I needed to be with someone who might be able to contact him. The mob had thinned out, and in the brief time we had, Skip drove through the iron gates, daring the guards to stop him, opened the door and The Girls and I dashed to the car for a fast ride to his home, a mile away. Somehow, Mike Tatosian had made it through to the Quarters before we left and was there to protect me, if necessary. When I left, he was standing in the middle of the cavernous living room with fireplace tongs and shovel, ready to fight off any invaders.

Holding a dog under each arm, I said, "Thanks, Mike. I'll never forget this."

He grinned. "It's my job. Now get going." We both knew it was more than that.

Through the night, Skip worked at his walkie talkie until I finally heard Jim's voice, cutting in and out.

"Bad connection, but I'm all right. Are you? Over."

"It's Patti. The Girls and I are with Skip and Shannon. Mike's at the Quarters.

I sent the Staff away."

I handed the receiver to Skip. "Admiral, can you get out of there? Over."

"Not now." Static. "…..mob all around the building. I'm going to make a run for it soon. Over."

The warrior was in his element.

Two long hours later, Jim's voice came through again. "I'm out and on my way to the office. Stay with the family. Over."

311

A shudder of relief went through me, but I knew I wouldn't see him until the next day. Heavy message traffic waited for him in his office at TDC.

On Monday, the students resumed their classes and an uneasy normalcy settled on us. A State Department team would come the second of January to formally break the Treaty and install a Cultural and Trade policy, instead. Wearily, I knew that meant more riots and worries about Jim's safety.

Christmas was an anti-climax. Despite our diminishing supply of food, we decided to have Jim's Staff and their families come to Quarters A for Christmas dinner. 'Naldo cleaned out the pantry and put together some interesting dishes no one could name. Skip had won a turkey –- an old Tom, probably stringy that looked too small to feed us all.

Jim eyed it grimly. "Maybe Mike can scrounge some things to add to it."

"Mike could find pheasant under glass if that's what we want."

We would make do and hopefully, provide a bright spot for an otherwise miserable holiday.

Two days before Christmas, the phone rang.

"Pat, it's Queenie Yao."

I was stunned. My dear friend Queenie held one of the highest positions in the Premier's office. "Queenie, you're the only one to call me. I don't know what to say." I could feel tears gathering.

Quietly, she said, "Pat, we love you."

That did it. I broke down. When I could speak again, I said, "I am so ashamed of what's happened and I can only pray you know how *we* feel."

"We do know. Goodbye for now, Pat."

It broke the dam. Gifts began arriving, flowers and of course, more Kaolien brandy. Two towering Christmas trees were delivered and I called down to Sgt. Hsiu, asking him to come help me get our packages into an official car. He was as happy as I, making the deliveries and the faces of our Chinese friends reflected Queenie's sentiments.

The parties resumed, but it was a highly emotional and difficult time. Ahead was the arrival of the delegation from the State Department and none of us were looking forward to that. Jim would meet the dignitaries at the airport, then escort them on the long journey through Taipei to the Grand Hotel where the talks would begin. The list was impressive: Warren Christopher, State Department, Richard Holbrooke, Assistant Secretary of State for Asian Affairs and an old friend, Admiral Maurice (Mickey) Weisner, Commander-in-Chief, Pacific. Accompanying them were high ranking Chinese military and government officials. The question was, what was the mood of Taipei? We were met with angry looks wherever we went and the house guards, now doubled in number, refused to salute Jim's official car when it came through the gates, giving us the suggestion of being under 'house arrest'.

More than ever before, we could not openly discuss events while at home. As Americans, it wasn't safe to go alone in our little car and phone calls were becoming non-existent because of the general knowledge that our phones were tapped. It was a lonely, frightening time. The Girls sensed something was wrong and stayed close to me all day long.

CHAPTER THIRTY FOUR

January 2 1979

The mob was waiting at the airport. The Girls and I sat on the floor of the sitting room, watching on television as the shiny, black limousines lined up to receive the delegation from the State Department, coming to break the thirty-year treaty. On a signal, the crowd attacked the cars as they began their journey to the Grand Hotel. Knowing which car held Jim and Admiral Weisner, I kept my eyes fastened on it. Rocks flew. Eggs, mud and tomatoes splattered against the windows, but it was the long, wooden sticks and metal pipes that would do the real damage and the younger members of the rioters held them ready.

A man in the crowd, reached into a brown paper sack and panicking, I called to Jim's shadowy face on the television screen. "Get down, Jim. He has a gun."

But the man's hand held peanuts and as a gesture of contempt toward our President, the peanut farmer from Georgia, he threw them at the official cars. A woman on her hands and knees crept between his widespread legs and picked them up. They were food and she had a family to feed.

By the time the limousines left the airport, they were all but destroyed. I had no idea if Jim was injured or even alive after watching metal pipes smash in the windows of the cars. It would be many hours before, exhausted and disheveled, he came back to the Quarters.

His eyes were on the mountains again as he wearily said, "Did you see the condition of the cars after we left the airport?"

"No Jim, I didn't. Apparently the media lost interest after the rioters dispersed. By the time the limos reached the end of the airport road, the coverage had ended."

"They should have stayed with us. It got worse downtown."

"Were they rioting against you there, too?"

"No, but the cars finally died and we had to get the group to the Grand Hotel intact."

"What did you do? I tried to lighten his day a little. "Call a cab?"

"As a matter of fact, we ducked into a hotel, then out a side door and hailed one that was across the street. Yeah, you might say we called a cab." We both laughed.

"We rendezvoused at the Grand Hotel and everyone made it safely. But the State Department bunch were very startled and you might say, upset at their reception in Taipei."

"What else did they expect? They've just pulled the rug out from under the ROC."

"Not what happe;ned. I think they just wanted to turn around and go home."

I detected a note of disgust in Jim's voice. I felt the same disgust as I thought about the danger he had been in.

Thinking my family would be frantic about our safety, I called my brother in Iowa only to find the American media had chosen to ignore the whole thing. He knew nothing about it and assumed I was homesick. I didn't enlighten him otherwise. Instead, I thanked God our children were safe in the United States.

February 1979

The business at hand was to pack up and move out. We would be the last to leave and anything of any value had to be listed, photographed and catalogued. I was glad for the activity. Instead of three years in Taipei, we had less than two, but after the past few weeks, I wanted only to get on a plane out and leave the stress behind.

It was the beginning of the end for Jim's Command. Twenty-three years of the Taiwan Defense Command had to be dismantled and disbanded in less than three months. Jobs had to be found for the Chinese nationals whose livelihood had depended on the U.S. government. Installations throughout the island would cease to exist, with other U.S. bases in the Pacific area taking whatever they could get. But most difficult of all, every American flag at our bases on the island would have to come down. Jim never thought he would lower the American flag in defeat and I saw it take its toll on him. Each day brought new crises until our nerves were raw.

With the Girls on either side of me, I sat on the porch in my nightgown, robe and slippers, alternating between reading the *Stars and Stripes* and studying the misty mountains that would forever remain in my thoughts.   An article told of the breaking of the Treaty and Carter's condemnation by the U.S.Congress for waiting until they were away from Washington for the Christmas holidays to carry out his dastardly deed.   Senator Barry Goldwater called it the 'most cowardly act by a President of the United States.'   Good to hear, but small comfort to a struggling democracy on the verge of annihilation.

Activity below the porch drew my eyes to the small shed that held our generator, at the foot of the driveway, It was the only source of power should the ROC government choose to cut off our electricity. They were undoubtedly angry enough to do it. A group of four men were in front of the shed, trying to break the lock.

Without hesitation, the Girls and I ran down the long flight of porch steps, robe flapping and yelling at the top of my lungs, ordering them to go away. As a group, they moved back a few paces and I used that space to fling myself across the door with arms outstretched.

"Bu hau, bu hau, bu hau," the Chinese word for 'bad'. It was my assessment of them all.

Once again, as a group, they left the premises, running up the driveway to get away from a crazy woman with murder in her eye. The Girls were beside themselves and Suzie chased the four up the driveway, barking and growling like bull mastiff. Boom Boom sat on my foot and muttered.

A social life of sorts set in. Farewell parties were the order of the day and they raged until we stepped on the plane. I noticed the Chinese ladies surreptitiously holding up one hand to each other, fingers spread. When I asked what it meant, they explained the five fingers meant they had five years left to live until the communists invaded Taiwan and killed them. I was horrified, questioned it and found that was their reality.

I have never felt more helpless.

Our furniture and car were gone, but I chose to remain at the Quarters as long as possible to be with The Girls, so we rattled around in a bare house. At last, The First Secretary of the South African Embassy took both Suzie and Boom Boom and they moved into a suite with their own garden at the Grand Hotel. The heart went out of me then and I agreed to move into the Hilton until time to leave. I saw them one more time.

One sunny March afternoon, Sgt. Hsiu drove me to the grounds of the Grand Hotel where I knew my little white dogs might be. As Sgt. Hsiu held the door for me, I stepped out and saw them immediately. They were chasing each other, but stopped when they became aware of the car. For just a moment, the two little white dogs hesitated, then became two white blurs as they ran into my arms. I held them as long as I could.

Even Sgt. Hsiu had tears in his eyes as I said goodbye to my Girls.

Our farewell party from the combined Chinese military was, to say the least, memorable. An opera had been composed, in our honor. But as we were dressing for this stellar event, Jim handed me one more shock.

Quietly, he said, "Patti, I'm going to retire after this tour of duty. Rather than a desk job in Washington, I want to do something different. I don't know what, but not this – not anymore." He was sitting in the wing chair, elbows on his knees, studying his hands. We were both dealing with disillusionment and the motivation to continue just wasn't there anymore. After a pause he said, "It's been thirty-six challenging years and I want to move on."

I understood his intentions. When I could find my voice again, I asked, "Are you sure?"

"Yes." The man of few words.

"I'm delighted, Jim. I couldn't be happier."

We went to the opera.

It was quite a night. After dinner, we were seated dead center on the first row in front of the large stage and surrounded by Chinese dignitaries and friends. To the accompaniment of clanging cymbals and banging drums 'Our opera' depicted the betrayal of the Republic of China by the United States and just to make sure we understood every word, an English interpreter at the side of the stage, made the message crystal clear. I sat next to Jim, hands folded in my lap, both feet squarely on the floor, eyes fixed on the stage and thought about retirement. Time for the children, time to do anything we *wanted* to, live where we chose, find that other world that so often seemed non-existent.

The smile on my face must have caused some wonderment among the members of the audience.

April 1979

It was over.

Skip and his family would leave on the plane after ours. He insisted on remaining with Jim until we left. The Navy, in one last swipe at us, informed Jim we must carry on our person, the Navy silver that had been part of Quarters A for twenty-three years; flatware, bowls, serving trays and platters. A trip to Tien Mou produced the necessary bags to pack it in and we left Taiwan with sixteen pieces of luggage, twelve of which, held Navy silver. It weighed more than I did.

We snorkeled our way across the Pacific by way of the various Micronesian Islands, healing as we went. Arriving on some tiny, remote island with sixteen pieces of luggage carried its own set of problems, but for the first time in such a long time, I felt free and although the retirement ceremony was yet to come, I was done.

The residue of Jim's command had been sent to Hawaii to meld into the major Pacific command, or CINCPAC. From Kwajalein, we flew into Honolulu at midnight. Because the pilot of the Air Micronesia could not get the nose wheel down, we circled the Pacific for nearly an hour, with instructions we would ditch in the ocean after the fourth and final pass over the runway. I knew the sixteen pieces of luggage full of Navy silver would take us straight to the bottom, and after what we had just been through in Taiwan I figured it was Fate.

We crash landed, were foamed from nose to tail and joyfully, thanked the pilot and God for getting us through one more near miss.

I knew there had to be one ordinary day out there somewhere. Maybe tomorrow.

Three days later, emergency surgery was performed on my left eye at Tripler Army Hospital. After living on the edge all during the Taiwan duty, the trauma of the plane crash caused the cornea to seal to the iris and without surgery within an hour, I would be blind. The buildup of fluid in my eye would blow the optic nerve. The head ophthalmologist surgeon was in the Micronesian Islands, treating native patients with cataracts, his Executive Officer had a broken arm and a very nervous young Lieutenant did major surgery on the Admiral's wife. He did it right.

I healed, took up oil painting and had the other eye done six weeks later.

Lying in the hospital bed for the second time, images formed on my mind:

A thin, frightened Jimmy Chen, out of job a at our TDC Boutique, crouched by the iron gates at Quarters A, begging our help.

The tears on Admiral Soong's cheeks as we cried together – he, in fear and sorrow for his country and I, in shame for mine.

The Methodist Missionary, who took my hand between hers and said, "I escaped from a Chinese communist prison after twenty years of solitary confinement. They *will* come."

The faces of the house Staff as I held each one, then let them go.

The tears on Sgt. Hsiu's face as we said goodbye at the airport.

But as the afternoon sun lay on the clipped green lawn of the hospital, through a haze of medicine, happier memories filtered through:

Suzie, with a potato chip in her mouth, heading for her favorite guard who played his guitar and sang to her.

The delicacy, a blackened chicken foot, stuck upright in a bowl of white rice and because of my Iowa background, my inability to pick it up and chew on it.

Lunch at the Ritz with my Chinese friends, dressed like Parisian fashion models and chattering to each other in their soft patois.

The plum tree at the foot of the lawn, first to flower in the spring and a testament to survival and hope.

As the medicine took over, the memories faded.

Patricia Linder

EPILOGUE

All that remained was the official ceremony of retirement. There was no Command to pass along to the next man. Jim chose to return to Norfolk where our home was and have a friend and Naval Academy classmate, Admiral Harry Train, officiate. Now that the decision was made, we wanted to get on with it.

Members of the Admiral's staff slipped into the room and I stood beside and slightly behind Jim as Harry read the words, separating Jim from thirty-six years of military service. I listened only to the words, keeping my mind a blank, rather than filling it with memories of those years.

A medal was pinned on Jim. How there could be room for any more was a mystery and the word 'Tilt' slipped into my thoughts. The dark blue and white of the Navy Cross remained alone at the top of the colorful bank of ribbons and my pride in his accomplishments never wavered.

I thought it was over. As I turned to Jim, the Admiral spoke. "Pat, I have something for you."

What's this? Was I to be handed yet another silver Revere bowl with an inscription on it? I was flustered and suddenly wished I were someplace else instead of rooted to the floor of Harry Train's office. He said words I don't remember. Then he pinned a medal on my dress.

As it should be for every Navy wife who stays the course.

Patricia Linder

ABOUT THE AUTHOR

Patricia Linder, award-winning writer, spent thirty-seven years, honing her talents to match the demands of her husband's naval career.

In *Row, Row, Row Your Boat*, her first memoir, she allows the reader to share with her the roller-coaster ride of a Navy wife, often alone, but always expected to be a 'woman for all seasons.'

Currently, she is working on her second memoir written about an explosive tour of duty in Taiwan, Republic of China toward the end of her husband's career.

The Linders moved to Tucson, Arizona eight years ago to be nearer their two children, Jamey and Jeffrey.

If you wish to contact the author, please use the residence address: 37865 South Spoon Drive, Tucson, Az. 85739 or e-mail: RowRowone@aol.com, Tel: 520-825-8335